D0850231

Letters from a World War I Aviator

Letters
from
A World War I
Aviator

BY JOSIAH P. ROWE, JR.

Collected and edited by Genevieve Bailey Rowe and
Diana Rowe Doran

Published by The Sinclaire Press
Boston, 1986

First printing: September, 1986
Second printing: February, 1987

For information: The Sinclaire Press, 42 Bay View Road, Wellesley,
Massachusetts 02181

Printed in the United States of America

Library of Congress Catalog Number 86-90456

ISBN 0-9616886-0-2

Table of Contents

Josiah P. Rowe Jr.
2nd Lt. A. S.

Preface

Attics in old family homes often yield treasures.

That is just what happened at the Rowe family home in Fredericksburg, Virginia, where I began my married life in 1921, and where I continue to live.

A number of years after my husband's death I discovered these letters tucked away in a corner of the attic. I immediately knew that they were a treasure to be preserved and so began the task of publication.

My venture into publishing, however, soon met with frustration and was abandoned for a long while. My daughter, Diana, came to my aid, and through her efforts, my dream has been realized.

Genevieve Bailey Rowe

Introduction

This collection of letters was written by my father during his tour of duty in World War I. An avid pilot and observer of the passing scene, his descriptions of camp life, side trips to such places as Rome and the Isle of Capri, and practice flights, as well as patrols along enemy lines, not only capture the spirit of the times but also show us something of his own ebullient nature. He returned from the war unscathed and went on to live an active and productive life in Fredericksburg.

He was born on October 8, 1894, in Fredericksburg at 801 Hanover Street, the family home since 1820. Christened Josiah Pollard Rowe, Jr., by his parents, Josiah Porter Rowe and Julia Taliaferro Rowe, he was the fifth of nine children.

Josiah attended the local Fredericksburg schools and was a student at Virginia Polytechnic Institute when the United States entered World War I. He enlisted in the army at Fort Myer, Virginia in 1917, graduated from the School of Military Aeronautics at Princeton University, and was sent overseas with the United States Air Service of the American Expeditionary Forces from October, 1917 through the end of the war.

Josiah received his preliminary flight training in Foggia, Italy and was commissioned a second lieutenant in May of 1918. He was then shipped to France where he received advanced combat flying training at Issoudon and aerial gunnery training at Cazaux. He joined the 147th Aero Squadron, First Pursuit Group, in Rembercourt where he flew in combat patrols until the end of the war.

Although 11,000 American aviators were trained during World War I, only a third were sent to Europe, and of this group only 600 were to see any combat at all. Josiah was one of the few and received the World War I Victory Medal with two battle clasps and two gold overseas chevrons.

A prolific writer, his letters home were printed in *The Daily Star*, where his uncle, A. P. Rowe, was editor. The readers of *The Star* responded warmly to these first-hand observations of war-time Europe.

Upon returning from the war, he returned to the family home and soon began working as advertising manager of *The Daily Star* and *The Free Lance*, which combined in 1926 to form *The Free Lance-Star*. In 1921, he married my mother, Genevieve Bailey, and they raised three children, Charles, Josiah and myself, at 801 Hanover Street.

Josiah's interest in flying continued well after the war, and he continued to maintain contact with his old squadron, attending a number of reunions over the years. Not long after his return from Europe, Josiah struck up a friendship with Sidney L. Shannon, a local resident who devised Fredericksburg's first airstrip and later its first and only airport. Sidney and Josiah both shared an abiding love of music, and Josiah became a member of Sid Shannon's Serenaders, playing both trombone and saxophone with the group at regional proms and social events. Coincidentally, Shannon was later to become Eastern Airlines' first vice president of operations, serving under Eddie Rickenbacker, the most victorious American aviator of World War I. Rickenbacker served in the First Pursuit Group in Rembercourt, France along with my father.

By the mid-1930s Josiah was to own his own plane, a single engine Curtiss Robin which he used primarily for pleasure though occasionally for business purposes such as meetings of the Virginia Press Association.

Introduction

His affiliation with The Free Lance-Star Publishing Company became his life's work. By 1925 he had risen to the dual position of manager and editor, and in 1947 he became the owner and publisher as well.

During World War II, Josiah helped organize Company 104 of the Virginia State Guard in which he served as its first commander with the rank of captain.

In 1948 he was to become the mayor of Fredericksburg, as both his father and grandfather before him, and his son Josiah after. His involvement with the newspaper business was one of strong commitment, and he served as president of the Virginia Press Association and state chairman of the Associated Press.

My brothers, Charles and Josiah, succeeded him as joint publishers of the paper upon his death in 1949. In later years, Charles continued his affiliation with industry associations by serving on the national board of directors of the Associated Press. My father's love of music had a major impact on my life, and as a child I began playing the piano in the front parlor at 801—thus commencing what was to become a lifelong avocation and sometime vocation.

The decision to publish these letters was embraced warmly, partly as a tribute to this dashing young airman, partly to introduce him to younger generations who never knew him, and partly as a reminder of this friend of many, both in and outside of the family.

Diana Rowe Doran

An Editorial Note

Editing an editor's letters can at first appear a daunting task. Here, the effort has been primarily a light dusting: misspellings have been corrected, errant commas redirected, and where doubt has interceded, the original informality remains intact.

The letters span the entire period that Josiah spent overseas, from the time that he shipped out on board the RMS *Adriatic* until the end of the war. A diary that he kept on board the *Adriatic* has been included here and is then followed by the letters.

In many of the letters there is no salutation, closing or signature, and this is partly because some of the letters were sent directly to *The Daily Star* and many were forwarded by his family to the newspaper which, in turn, deleted this material. In most instances, it was the newspaper articles, not the original letters, that survived.

In addition to being a prolific letter-writer, Josiah took hundreds of photographs from the time that he left New York in 1917 until the end of the war. All but two of the photographs reproduced in this book were taken from his collection or albums. The captions that appear in quotation marks were written by Josiah.

To assist in clarifying references throughout, a nominal amount of footnoting has been used—as much to let younger generations know who or what is being discussed as to assist older ones with the general process of remembering. While the footnotes are generally considered sound, they are largely a matter of human recollection. In the interest of speeding publication, the recollections are assumed to be correct, although some errors may well exist.

Specific military information in the introduction, footnotes, and addenda was provided by Col. Clarence Richard Glasebrook, United States Air Force, a military historian with a special interest in the aviators of World War I, and, coincidentally, a close friend of Ken Porter, Josiah's flight commander at the Front in France. Col. Glasebrook reviewed the manuscript, provided answers to many questions, and wrote the overview of the Air Service which appears in the addenda. He and his wife, Millie, who assisted him, were enthusiastic supporters of this project, for which we are most appreciative. Sadly, Col. Glasebrook died July 7, 1986, just as the book was going to press.

On Board
the RMS *Adriatic*

1917

Tuesday, Oct. 23—Princeton, N.J.[1]*—6 p.m.*—Ordered to pack up and leave for Mineola[2] the next day; sounds like France; big hurry; kept wires hot saying good-bye; also wrote farewell letters.

Wednesday, Oct. 24—Heavy rain and very cold. Left Princeton at 1:15. Reported at Mineola at 6 P.M.—cold, wet, and sloppy—no accommodations for us, so left baggage and returned to New York. Saw *Oh! Boy,* went to the Black Cat and had a large night.

Thursday, Oct. 25—Reported at Mineola at 9:30. Everything in confusion. Expected to leave with previous classes which were packing up, but when issued cots and blankets and assigned to quarters we gave up hope and were prepared for about ten days' "rest cure." Loafed around all day; told other crowd good-bye.

Friday, Oct. 26—Loafed all day, except for putting in clothing requisition. A million conflicting rumors afloat all based on hearsay and conjecture. Can't get pass to New York. Enjoy watching planes, twelve to fifteen in the air at a time. Rotten food and poor sanitary arrangements.

[1]The ground school that Josiah attended was the U.S. School of Military Aeronautics at Princeton University.

[2]Mineola, New York (on Long Island), site of an army flying field.

Saturday, Oct. 27—8:30 A.M.—Told to pack up and leave in 15 minutes, which we did. Fell in with detachments from ground schools at Boston Tech, Ohio State, Georgia Tech, Cornell, and Univ. of Illinois. Wild ride on motor trucks across Long Island through New York to pier where we boarded the steamer *Adriatic,* White Star Line. Awfully dismal feeling with not a soul to whom I could say good-bye. Were not allowed to go on shore, and of course I thought of thousands of things I needed but am glad now that I didn't get them as I can probably get nearly everything in London very much cheaper. Steamed out from the dock at 3 o'clock but were made to stay indoors while in the harbor; looked through the windows for the last glimpse of the Singer Building, Woolworth Building, Battery, Governor's Island, and the Statue of Liberty. Beautiful afternoon and everybody comes out on deck. We are always at the mercy of God but I never felt so much so as when we dropped the pilot and shortly after got our last glimpse of land. But for the swiftness of events and the novelty of the experiences I would have been terribly blue. . . . The *Adriatic* is a wonderful ship—a perfect monster of wood and steel—about ten years old but quite modern in every respect. We have first-class passage, and the accommodations are magnificent—every possible comfort and convenience—elevators, Turkish bath, swimming pool, gymnasium, spacious lounge and saloon, and a peach of a bar and smoking room. The bar is an unhoped for luxury, and everyone patronizes it liberally. Oh! What a joy to sit in your stateroom and have the steward bring down the most delicious drinks! While the drinks are not expensive, I fear that some of the men, who are so thankful at finding such an oasis, will be broke before we reach the other side. . . . There are about 100 student aviators and about as many officers. This much of warfare hasn't been so bad and I am beginning to doubt the famous statement of Sherman.[3] Feel sorry for the 2,000 enlisted men (Signal Corps, and N. G. Inf.) down below—poor devils, they get the rough end of everything and always have the dirty work to do. At dusk, every porthole, window and door is covered with black curtain so that not a glimmer is visible from the outside. Only two doors are used for exits and these are at the end of dark hallways. Glorious moonlight and calm sea—can't stand it out on deck, makes me think too much about home and . . . so I go down to smoker and drink to their health and forget them—temporarily.

Sunday, Oct. 28—Rise at 8:30, have bath and breakfast at 9. Beautiful day, warm and clear. Have church services conducted by surgeon. The singing of the good old hymns touched me deeply, especially when we sang one verse of "My Country, 'Tis of Thee" and one of "God Save the King." About a dozen English officers on board, all young and congenial—one Lt. Col. of the Royal Flying Corps who is a peach. Also several English civilians and wives, all middle-aged—not a young woman on the ship. Got a wireless from Arlington telling of the success of the Liberty Loan, and of the Italian reverses. Seems strange to have spent the summer within a stone's throw of Arlington, hearing the buzz at nights, and now to be a thousand miles away picking up its messages. It is reported that we go to Liverpool, stopping at Halifax, Nova Scotia, but am not certain. Big talk of submarines with some quite skeptical about our chances of evading them. Rumored that Lloyds is betting 50 to 1 against this ship reaching England which sounds to me like "bunk." *Adriatic* is known as The Munition Queen and it seems that the Germans are anxious to get her. She is loaded with ammunition and has 12 big

[3]"War is hell," a statement made by Union General William Tecumseh Sherman a number of years after the Civil War.

3

howitzers for Russia, but she is fast (18 knots), has a 3-inch gun mounted on her stern, and will be convoyed, so prospects are favorable. Spend afternoon in deck chair, reading and sleeping. Write letters at night in hopes of mailing them in Halifax.

Monday, Oct. 29—On deck by 9—quite cold and it looks as if my old friend B.V.D. is going to lose a good fight. Land in sight—very bleak and desolate but as we approach the harbor appearances are more cheerful and inviting. Coast is hilly and covered with fir trees—can see neat looking settlements along shore. All is quiet and peaceful and it is hard to imagine the whole world being at war. See smoke rising from homes and sail boats skimming along—very striking picture—am reminded of Emerson's (?)—

> The morning's at seven,
> The hilltop's dew pearled;
> God's in his heaven,
> All's well with the world.

Anchor at Halifax about 11 o'clock but not allowed to go ashore. Harbor is well protected from submarines by steel nets and chasers. Can see about 12 ships, liners and battleships, presumably of our fleet. Some of them are grotesquely daubed with paint of various colors which break up the outlines and make them much less visible. Can see some of the town though it is obscured by hills—looks like about 75,000. Reported that we may stay a week or longer. Get local newspapers but they are very poor. . . . The bar is growing in popularity—only one man has refused a drink so far and he misunderstood the question. You never have to look in but one place to find anyone. . . . Some of the officers complain of the lack of proper respect on the part of the cadets, which claim is absolutely unfounded. It is customary when on ship to salute only once a day but they contend that the salute is an honor to which they are entitled at all times. What matters time-honored custom and convention when they have commissions, and some have actually had them about two weeks!! Some of them don't know yet how to wear their insignia, and shoulder straps don't make an officer but they are our superiors (?) and we must obey their commands. Besides the ex-National Guard, most of them are ground officers in the Aviation Section, and when we get our commissions we will [out]rank them all. At any rate, they are on top now and if they want salutes they shall have them.

Tuesday, Oct. 30—Started before breakfast with salutes—concerted action. We always go in a skirmish line of two's or three's and just far enough apart so that our victims will have to return each salute separately. It's fun to catch them unsuspectingly smoking a cigar, to slip up beside them quickly and watch them hurriedly jerk them out of their mouths, usually breaking the cigar or burning their fingers. Sometimes we catch them with both hands occupied and then their movements are ludicrous. They want salutes and they shall have them but I shouldn't be surprised if they don't get sick of the nuisance before very long. Beautiful day but just lying in the harbor is getting monotonous. Two U.S. battleships go out which gives rise to the hope that we may leave soon. Have lifeboat drill, which needs lots of practice. There are about 3,000 persons on board and it requires a good system to get them all in lifeboats in ten minutes. Judging from today's performance, the submarine would have to give us about 30 minutes warning if we are to get away from the ship before she sinks. The greatest menace is the possibility of a panic but if the troops have been properly disciplined, there shouldn't be any danger. There are four pianos on board and about every other person plays, so we have an abundance of music.

Wednesday, Oct. 31—Lovely day and those who aren't playing poker in the smoker are on deck pitching quoits. No indications of leaving but at 3:30 we hoist anchor and steam out followed by all the other ships. There are eight ships in the fleet—no convoy yet—and they go out in line then take up formation—we being in the center, which is an important factor of safety in case of attack by U-boats. Traveling very slow—about 10 knots—on account of some of the smaller vessels. Entire fleet zig-zags continually. At this rate it looks like a voyage of about two weeks. Wonderful moonlight and great music on deck with ukes. Hallowe'en—celebrated by simple decorations in saloon. Concert in lounge by troops from below. . . . Lots of confab about our destination and the "dope" is that we land (submarines permitting) and train in the camp at Southampton. Sea a little rough and ship heaving noticeably. Evidences of sickness and some take refuge in bunks. Said that the best preventative is a hearty appetite well utilized—so there's no chance in the world of my being sick.

Thursday, Nov. 1—Stood watch from 4 to 5 A.M., cold, drizzly rain and very dark. The other ships about 200 yards distant are just blurs. Couldn't possibly see a submarine at more than ten yards but there is satisfaction in knowing that they likewise would have difficulty in seeing us. Can now appreciate fully the horrible brutality—the cold-bloodedness of deliberate murder by the Germans in torpedoing ships. It's bad enough in the daytime but in the dead of night it is something ghastly. It gives me the cold shivers to think of the horror of it. If a submarine should happen to spot us on such a night we would be at their mercy. Our greatest protection is darkness. I almost hope that we shall run into a squadron of U-Boats and that we can destroy every d----- one of them. . . . Rain all day so get in some good time reading. Have calisthenics on deck in the afternoon.

Friday, Nov. 2—Am acquiring Papa's habit of having a cup of coffee before rising. I didn't know it was so nice or I might have started the practice sooner. The reputation of the English in regard to tea isn't true on this boat but they are certainly strong for the coffee. They couldn't possibly get up in the morning without a cup and at 4 every afternoon coffee and sandwiches are served, while it is also an essential of every meal. After the hot eye-opener, a plunge in the cold sea water in the Turkish bath is a great appetizer and just makes you feel like you could lick a battleship. Still raining, so read nearly all day. Enjoyed *The Story of a Round House* by Masefield. Poker is going strong and is almost universally played. By the time we reach England, there will be about ten multi-millionaires and the rest dead broke. . . . Stood watch from 11 to 12 P.M., cold, wet and dark. There isn't much sport in standing out in the rain in one spot for an hour looking for submarines. You strain your eyes, and in every whitecap you think you see a periscope. Every minute you aren't humming a tune, you think of everyone you know and wonder what they are doing—and then you see something black right beside the ship which makes you tingle right down to the toes. There is a purse of £20 for anyone who sights a submarine in time to evade it and every cadet has already figured out just how he will spend it. Am getting to be quite an expert with the English currency, and it doesn't take more than eight minutes to calculate how much "One and Six" or "Two and Four" is. The English bills look like the profit sharing coupons you get in the United Cigar Stores.

Saturday, Nov. 3—Still raining and very foggy. They say this is the weather you nearly always have in England—if so send me to Egypt. A little sunshine would be worth a million dollars. . . . We certainly have the officers on the run now. They can't enjoy a walk around the deck any more and their reading is made miserable by interruptions. They try to avoid us but we hunt them down and pester them to death. Some of them are good sports and join in our games and arguments but others don't deign to notice us—only they have to return a salute and believe me they will be good at it when this voyage is over. The "All Out" alarm was just sounded and we were out on deck with life-belts in about 11 seconds. They just wanted to be certain that we hadn't forgotten it. Have been on board ship just a week with indications of another and then some—this "speed" of ours is killing.

Sunday, Nov. 4—RAIN—Attended church services and spent the day in reading and sleeping. Just learned that one of the ships with us is a battle-cruiser with hidden guns which was very comforting news, only there are miles of room for a submarine to operate without getting too close to her guns, and besides all the ships have guns but what good will they do after the torpedo has been fired?

Monday, Nov. 5—Heavy wind all day and sea getting rough. At night it develops into a regular storm. Stood watch from 3 to 4 A.M., and honestly had to hold on to the rail to keep from being blown or pitched off. The ship just tossed about like a toy boat and it was impossible to sleep. The storm wasn't as fierce as those one reads about but it was quite enough for me.

Tuesday, Nov. 6—Storm still raging and numerous ones are not feeling their best. Fellows are getting the flying fever again—the events of the voyage made us forget aeroplanes for a while but the spell is gripping us stronger than ever as we near the place where we are to begin work. . . . The attitude of the men and officers on board certainly presents an interesting study in psychology. With few exceptions, they seem to look upon this expedition as a frolic—more of a sight-seeing tour than, as it really is, a fight to the death with the Germans. Some appear to think more of matters of dress and plans for joy parties in Paris than they do of the more grim aspects of war. In spite of the way the English discount the ability of the Germans, they are still a powerful foe, and I fear that the United States is going to get some hard jolts before they realize just what they are up against. I know it would make the Germans laugh to see some of our "warriors" but I am sure they will show the right kind of stuff when the test comes.

Wednesday, Nov. 7—Cloudy, and storm dying down. Had lifeboat drill in morning. We are now in the danger zone and even more careful precautions are taken. Everybody has a tense feeling and even the slamming of a door makes one jump. At night there is more wind and rain and heavy darkness. The other ships are just phantoms. I am sick of rain but thank God for the pitch darkness. . . . It is funny to observe the contrast between the inside and outside of the ship—the lounge and smoker are ablaze with light; pianos, guitars and ukes are making merry music; the smoker is crowded with men drinking, smoking, and gambling, and having the best of fun, apparently oblivious to the dangers of the present and those of the immediate future. One could easily imagine himself in a club or hotel in New York. Then, just step outside on deck, and there isn't a gleam of light nor a sound except the blowing of the wind and the splashing of the waves. This gaiety may seem strange but I think it is all right—there isn't any use putting on a long face and bemoaning the fact that a torpedo may strike at any moment, blasting away the side of the ship—all the worry in the world will not prevent it. Then, too, these men have untold hardships and sufferings to endure, so why not enjoy some little pleasure while one is able?

On board R.M.S. *Adriatic*
Thursday, November 8, 1917

My dearest Mother and Papa and all:

We expect to land sometime Saturday and I want to write to you before this trip is over as I don't know what chances I will have for some little time.

Our voyage has been excellent so far in spite of the most disagreeable weather. It has been cloudy every day with considerable rain, and we have had just about four hours sunshine. The first day out I paid $1.00 for the use of a steamer chair, but it has been so cold and wet that I only used it one afternoon. However, there has been an abundance of things to do on the inside in the way of reading, writing and playing cards, so time has passed very quickly. On Monday and Tuesday we had what I thought was a regular storm but the oldtimers just scoffed at it. It was quite enough for me with mountainous waves tossing the big ship around like a toy, doing the corkscrew twist one minute and a swan dive the next. When one wished to go to bed all you had to do was to stand in the door of your stateroom and wait until the bed came around to you and then hop on. Some of the men will not forget it shortly, but I managed to live through it without "losing" anything but a little sleep.

We have been constantly on guard against submarines but now that we are in the danger zone the precautions are doubled. We have to do lookout duty for an hour each day and if there were really as many U-boats as we imagine we see there wouldn't be a chance of our reaching England. It is not any too comfortable a feeling when you know that they are looking for us, and that any minute a torpedo may blast away the whole side of the ship. We have gotten so now that every time a door slams or something falls, we unconsciously jump for our life belts.

Far be it from me to get nervous over such a little thing, but it would bring joy to my heart to get a glimpse of our convoy, and still more to see what good hard land looks like again.

We expect to land at Liverpool (submarines permitting) but have no idea where we will go for training—England, France or Italy. If the weather of the past two weeks is a sample of what they have in England, then I'm going to put in a bid for Egypt.

I have just attended a meeting of the Masons on board, and it was a most extraordinary meeting. There were men from England, Scotland, Ireland, Canada, and nearly every state in the Union.

Friday, November 9th—Oh! Joy, we can see the _____[1] and with glasses the _____. Also—Heaven be praised—a fleet of destroyers has just come out to meet us which gives us a wonderful feeling of relief. Now, there is some chance of this reaching you provided the censor is feeling well when he goes over it.

Will probably land this afternoon and have to start packing up pretty soon. I don't know how I'm to do it as I was loaded when I started, and Uncle Sam has kindly donated since some blankets and heavy underwear which has been a blessing. I can't pack it anywhere but you bet I am not going to leave it behind.

I will never get over the feeling upon leaving without being able to tell a soul goodbye, and I never thought so much of home as I do now. I hated to leave on such a long journey with so little preparation as there were so many things that I had left undone, especially around home, and I can't bear to think of even the slightest possibility of not

[1]A blank indicates that the military censor was presumably at work.

getting back to correct and complete my affairs. But I mustn't be blue, and you must not worry at all about me. Everything is going to come out all right, and with the knowledge of your prayers I always feel a sense of security.

My best love to everybody in the family—Clarkie[2] and Carpenter[3]—Mable[4] and Foster[5]—all the neighbors, friends and relatives. I hope Taylor[6] and Julia Mason[7] are doing their best at school, and that the girls aren't teaching Clarkie any bad habits. Tell Reg[8] that he has got to do the "loving" for both of us now, that is until I get located over here. Please write often and have Miss Nannie McCleary[9] send me *The Star.*

Devotedly,

Josiah

[2]Julian Clark, a boarder at 801 Hanover Street.

[3]A boarder at 801 Hanover Street.

[4]Mable Foster was then dating Josiah's brother Hansford Herndon Rowe (1893–1945). She was a student at the State Normal School (now Mary Washington College).

[5]Foster Taliaferro, a cousin. Also a friend of Mable Foster and a student at the Normal School.

[6]Taylor Prescott Rowe, a brother (1901–1981).

[7]Julia Mason Rowe, a sister (1903–1986).

[8]Reginald Thompson Rowe, a brother (1897–1951).

[9]An employee of *The Daily Star* and a boarder at 801 Hanover Street.

In Italy

Campo d'Aviazione, Sud
Foggia, Italy
November 28, 1917

To *The Daily Star*:

There are so many things that I want to tell the people of Fredericksburg that I don't know where to begin, and maybe what I do say won't get by the censor; but I am going to make an attempt to tell some of the things that have happened on this very wonderful trip.

We landed in Liverpool on Saturday, Nov. 9th, and after several hours waiting at the docks, took a train for Southampton. As we had only two hours of daylight we saw but little of the country, but what we did see was just as I had expected—only more so. The principal streets of the town were quite clean and orderly, but the side streets were narrow, dirty and crowded just like the ideas you get from Dickens' stories. The houses were all of brick about a thousand years old and two stories high and practically all just alike. The country was practically level or gently rolling, the fields green like spring or with the brown color of freshly cultivated earth, and trees were very conspicuous by their almost total absence. Every inch of ground was under cultivation.

The people greeted us enthusiastically all along the route and at every stop curious crowds would gather quickly at the mention of "Americans." Before leaving the ship we had been given lunch boxes, and at one station, just as we were opening them, a little fellow stuck his head in the door and asked, "Have you any white bread? We haven't had any for two years." You never saw anyone so delighted when we gave him some rolls. I might add that we haven't seen any white bread since that day. We passed a hospital train which gave us a distinct shock and made us realize that we were not out on a lark. After passing through Birmingham, Oxford and other towns we arrived at Southampton, left our baggage at the station (the last time we saw it) and walked three miles to a camp. That walk was anything but cheerful—not a soul on the streets, every window curtained and even the street lights shaded, so as to give the Boche[1] planes as much difficulty as possible in locating the towns. Except for the few very dim lights I was reminded of Goldsmith's *Deserted Village*. The night was quite cold and sleep in tents on boards with only two thin blankets was impossible. When morning and a little warmth finally came we had the pleasure of breakfast which some of the men kindly shared with us.

After loafing all morning we formed at noon and marched through town to the docks and after three hours more of waiting boarded a small channel steamer—our baggage and a detail of men in charge following on another steamer. We were equipped with life belts and the possibility of being torpedoed was the main topic of conversation. Going out of the harbor just before dark we expected to find the channel quite rough, but on the contrary it was as calm as could be. The boat was small and fast, but it was never intended for night trips, for there was absolutely no provision for sleeping and we were so crowded that even by stretching out on the floor we couldn't get room enough. We had been out about two hours when we came dangerously near colliding with a French aeroplane which had met with a mishap and fallen into the water. The pilot

[1]German.

16

was barely hanging on to the top wing and when he saw us bearing down on him he shouted. We flashed a few signals and almost instantly lights began blinking on every side and from out of the darkness five or six torpedo boats came sliding up without a sound with their flashlights playing all over the horizon. One of the gunboats came in close and picked up the pilot and machine and then with all dark and silent again we resumed our trip. We spent a miserable night, disembarking at Havre (France) early next morning.

On the march to a second "rest camp" we saw hundreds of German prisoners at work on the docks, streets and railroad yards, and their appearance was a flat contradiction to the reports of how Germany is starving. Every one of them was a husky specimen with a full, ruddy face and there was no outward indication of his having suffered any privations. Nevertheless, most of them seemed to prefer their lot as prisoners to that of soldiers in the trenches.

Just for fun we greeted some of the Germans with "wie gehts" which they returned jovially, pleased that we should speak with them. Whenever we would approach a group of them at work they would all stop and stare at us with a smile that might mean anything. I wondered what were their emotions at seeing us, but I think for the most part their faces expressed disdain and contempt.

We left Havre at 6 A.M. the next morning for Paris— even the mention of that name gave us a thrill.

The trip was very interesting although the country was not nearly so attractive as England. Stopping at nearly every station we were warmly greeted by soldiers and civilians alike. Our "Bon Jours," "A la Cartes" and "Bon Amis" were warmly returned. Many of the fellows could speak French fairly well and acted as interpreters. We reached Paris at 4 P.M. and were taken to barracks in town and told that we could either stay there or at a hotel until next morning. Although we had but little money the building was so dirty that everyone went down town.

A party of five of us went to the first hotel we could reach—the Elysée Palais, being about the most expensive in Paris, as we found out afterwards. But it was worth anything we had to get cleaned up for the first time since leaving the good old SS *Adriatic* at Liverpool. After spending several hours in the barber shop and bathtub we felt human again.

At night we went to an English vaudeville show, but the best show of all was right on the streets. While everything was greatly subdued there was gaiety in abundance and crowds and crowds of people. Some of the cafes were going full blast and life there was anything but serious. The people were extremely polite and would go to any limit to help us. When we would ask to be directed to any place they would not only tell us with much gusto, but insisted on showing us in person, no matter how far it might be. One night we stayed at the University Club, where we had excellent accommodations at very reasonable prices. At the University Club I met none other than Dr. Henry Van Dyke, former U.S. Minister to Holland, who introduced me at his bank so that I was enabled to draw some money against my delayed salary.

For real beauty Paris is absolutely unsurpassed. Everything that you have ever read about Paris—and some that you haven't—is true. I was deeply impressed when we went to see the Bastille and more so at the tomb of Napoleon.

The people are certainly fascinating. White uniforms for men and black for the women were almost universally worn and you could see that though the weight of war bore heavily upon them, they didn't take matters so seriously as the English. Their gaiety and frivolity were only on the surface and you could tell that under it all they were hiding untold suffering. At times I was sorry that I wasn't more familiar with French, but then it was lots more fun trying to speak it. The words we couldn't speak we could indicate by gesticulations, and one's delight when they would finally understand us was great.

We left Paris about 9 P.M. and awoke next morning in the heart of the most beautiful and picturesque mountains in the world. I wish I could describe to you the wondrous sights of the towering peaks covered with snow, and the magnificent scenes of the massive hills on every side. Far up some of the hillsides would be an ancient castle crumbling in ruins and there were countless homes which looked as if they might tumble down anytime.

At the last stop in France we had to go through customs inspection before entering Italy, but having lost our baggage somewhere between England and France we didn't have anything to be inspected. On the next stage of the journey, instead of going between the mountain ranges we went through them. There were some tunnels that seemed endless and then there would be a succession of short ones and we would get just a flash of light and then darkness. As the parts of the Alps and Appenines which we saw were so wonderful I am certainly going to Switzerland some day and see the Alps proper.

Soon we began to leave the mountains behind and as we came upon broad stretches of plains and vineyards and fruit orchards we knew we were in Italy. The land was well cultivated and looked very productive, but the homes spoke of nothing but poverty. On arriving at Torino we detrained and after marching to quarters all went down town for supper. You never saw curiosity as was displayed when the people learned that we were "Americano." Most of the time we were taken for English, but whenever possible we corrected that idea. It was very embarrassing to be stared at the way we were and whenever we would stop, a crowd would congregate in such a way that we would have to elbow our way through. If anything, the people were even more polite than in France. At first we found great difficulty with the language, but later with the aggregate knowledge of French, Latin, Spanish possessed by our party, and with the aid of gestures we could express our wants and partly understand the people. They are very much like the French, talking very fast and making frantic motions to express themselves.

Torino is a city of about 300,000, rather pretty but about 50 years behind time in most things. A world's exposition was held here some years ago and the buildings are still standing. There were plenty of stores and nearly everything could be bought at absurdly cheap prices. For instance a supper of the best Italy could offer cost about 4 lire (80¢). We visited an old castle on the banks of the Po River, of which century I don't know, but it surely was ancient and in a perfect state of preservation. There was the moat, the swinging bridge, iron door, high walls and towers, the courtyard, rooms for all the various operations of feeding and clothing the inmates, underground dungeons, dining rooms, bedrooms, and finally the throne room. All the living rooms had fantastic paintings (on the walls) and unreadable heiroglyphics. There was also the arsenal with all kinds of armor and weapons for fighting. It was all so ancient that I felt as if I were reading a story and could fancy the king, queen and other characters right there. But with everything so old and mouldy even a vivid imagination could not picture the princess.

In Torino are the great Fiat works, whence came the best automobile ever made—now engaged in making aeroplanes. Our route on leaving Torino was through Alessandria and Bologna, then right along the coast of the Adriatic Sea, through some wonderful agricultural regions, miles and miles of fig trees, orange trees and vineyards. For two days we traveled through this pretty country, then started inland where the country got gradually poorer and poorer until we reached Foggia—the backyard of civilization. I won't attempt to describe it, but suffice it to say that it is very, very old and very, very dirty and the people are very, very poor.

The camp is about 1½ miles from town, very nicely arranged and in an excellent location. It was full of flyers before we arrived so we have to kill time while watching the other fellows fly. However, we expect to get started in a few days and have our fun playing leapfrog with the clouds.

On good days the air is full of machines and it is tantalizing to watch the other fellows sailing around while we just sit in the sun and read. The Italian instructors are very efficient and cautious and have never had an accident. The school is conducted entirely by Italians, but there are a number of U.S. officers here in charge of us. I found Abe Carrington the first day and it was mighty good to see another Fredericksburger.

We go into town nearly every afternoon to break the monotony and as soon as we reach there we are attacked by crowds of children of both sexes begging for pennies. They try to catch hold of our hands, or hang on our coattails and it is almost impossible to get rid of them. Somebody made an awful mistake in giving them the first penny and now they are an abominable pest. When anyone drops a cigarette "butt" about eight of them dive for it and have a lively scramble in which heads get bumped, fingers stepped on and the few clothes they wear torn. It's really a picnic to watch them; but, as people here are radically opposed to the war, they are inclined to be hostile to us, and I am always afraid of getting into a row with somebody's daddy.

Throughout Italy foodstuffs are scarce, especially sweets; two days a week are "meatless." At the camp the mess, which is run by Italians, includes macaroni twice a day, every day, the only variety being in the length into which it is cut and the quantity of water used in cooking it. Still we are doing very well.

We are in great need of reading matter. The ten or twelve books in camp have a waiting list of about 20 and the few magazines have been read and re-read. You see we are absolutely removed from anything American—the only things in town of American manufacture being Singer sewing machines, Waterman fountain pens and Standard Oil.

Thus far I have seen nothing of the war zone, but on every opportunity I have talked to the English, French and Italian soldiers. They think we are in for at least two more years of fighting, for Germany is far from starving and she is still very powerful now that Russia has collapsed. It is up to the United States to keep up the spirit of the allies and help deliver the knockout blow. That time is a long way off, but we will lick the Hun eventually.

I am hoping that this will reach America by Christmas and I wish for *The Free Lance* and *Star* and all Fredericksburg a merry Christmas and a happy New Year.

In Italy

Campo d'Aviazione, Sud
Foggia, Italy
December 19, 1917

There hasn't been much of interest since my last letter, but this is such a beautiful day and there were so many things that I didn't mention before that I will write a line or two while enjoying the wonderful sunshine. I can't make myself believe it is so near Christmas—the weather is just like Indian summer and instead of holly and evergreen trees there are only fig and orange trees. We surely did have a fine taste of cold weather last week; it was very cold and damp and one day it snowed, a most extraordinary event in this section. We are living in stone barracks and on account of a dearth of fuel have no heat at all. There isn't a place in the whole camp to get warm, there being hardly enough wood for the kitchen, and it is a wonder everyone of us did not have pneumonia. I think our "winter" is about over now, as the last few days have been glorious and fine headway was made with flying. I have a good instructor, but he cannot speak English, although he makes frantic efforts to explain things to us. It really doesn't matter much as no amount of explanation will make an aviator; he has to do the flying himself and if something is done wrong the instructor immediately corrects it and you know you mustn't do that again. On our line they have a roundabout way of finding out what the instructor is trying to say. He tells the "motoriste" (mechanic) in Italian, the "motoriste" puts it into Spanish and tells one of the students who then passes it on to the others in English. But really these Italians don't need more than eight or ten words for a language—you can understand them almost perfectly by watching their facial expressions and the gestures of their arms. A very large proportion of the soldiers, both here and those we met at other places, have been to America and they love to talk about it. We ask them where they were, and no matter whether it was New York, Chicago or Philadelphia, we say we live there and it just tickles them to death. Believe me, they aren't going to lose any time getting back to the States after this war and they will carry many others with them.

To get back to flying, it is the most wonderful sensation in the world—you don't know what a real thrill is until you go shooting through space at 90 miles an hour with the whole world spread out beneath you. I am just itching for the day when I can fly alone, without an instructor who wants everything done his way. It looks as if we will be here at least six months doing flying that would not take a month if it were not for the congestion. We must have 25 lessons with an instructor before going to "solo" and then after various tests and cross-country flights alone we go on the Caproni[1] for training in bombing. We average a lesson a day on the field until all flying for the day is over. There has been a minimum of accidents here, so far none of a serious nature, but the extremely cautious Italians are always worried and sometimes they get fearfully angry. A rather queer thing happened the other day—one of the students went up for his altitude test about 3 P.M., going up about 16,000 feet, far up above the clouds, where it was bright as day, or rather it was daylight up there. Upon coming down below the clouds about 5 P.M. it was quite dark. He couldn't see how to land but luckily guessed when he was close to the ground. Everything would have been all right except for a farm house, which got in the way. The plane was smashed to splinters, but the fellow didn't

[1] A tri-motor airplane used as a bomber.

24

get a scratch. He stayed up too long and forgot that the higher you go the longer the sun is visible. It gets dark here very quickly on account of the mountains.

We are still enjoying such delicacies as boiled macaroni and sour potatoes. That Thanksgiving supper I spoke of was a fake—rooster and bologna sausage full of garlic. The food would not be so bad if it were cooked halfway decently, but they just put it on the stove and let it take care of itself. After a certain time it is considered ready. They have absolutely no idea of seasoning, using grated cheese in everything. Whenever we have a friend or can make a "raise" we go into town and try to get something good, but even there we fail. The best cafe in town isn't near as good as the Athens[2] at home and it seems that every time I go in it is a meatless day: it's a mighty good thing I like eggs. No matter what you order they always bring a dish of macaroni and I can handle it like an expert now. The Jews may be good as merchants, but they can't compare with these Italians. If they ask 10 lire for an article, offer them 5 and they will still be making a handsome profit. There is a war tax on everything from a cake of soap to a theatre ticket. The Americans have run prices up so that the Italian soldiers who get two cents a day can't buy a thing any more. We still have hopes of getting paid some day and we will make half as much again on exchange from American currency to Italian, but the shopkeepers get the benefit—not us.

We are still in dire straits regarding literature. Have read every book in camp—good or bad. By being off in this godforsaken corner of Italy we are detached from the headquarters base and get the benefit of the Y.M.C.A.'s Christmas packages or tobacco funds. American cigarettes are worth $1.00 a piece and the fellow who gets any has

[2]A popular restaurant at the former Athens Hotel in Fredericksburg.

to guard them with his life. In a movie show one night they showed a picture of New York's skyline and we nearly had a riot.

The world isn't so big after all, is it? Today I was talking to one of the boys in my room and I will give you one guess who he was. His name is Kerr,[3] lives in Baltimore, went to Wisconsin, belonged to Dixie Club and knew Charles[4] well, has a brother at Johns Hopkins, who is a great friend of George.[5] He knows George, too, and also met Taylor when he was there in the spring. He came over with the first detachment and is now nearly through his training. He is a capital fellow and thought the world of Charles, also spoke very highly of George. There is also a chap named Greenbaum[6] from Pittsburgh, who has been to Fredericksburg often, being connected with A. Leo Wiel, of Tidewater. Also Krogstad,[7] of Washington, who has visited Count d'Adhemar and the Embreys. Strange that I should meet these fellows way over here.

Rah! Rah! The commandant just announced that we could have three days leave Christmas to go either to Rome or Naples. Gee! I have to pinch myself to see if I am awake. I can't realize that historic Rome and scenic Naples are within 100 miles and that within a few days I shall be in one of them. I think I shall go to Naples, as it is warmer there and I will get a chance to go to Rome upon completion of my second Brevet Tests[8] (corresponding to Reserve

---

[3] 1st Lt. Spencer H. Kerr.

[4] Charles Spurgeon Rowe, a brother (1891–1915).

[5] George Davis Rowe, a brother (1889–1978).

[6] 2nd Lt. Meyer Greenbaum.

[7] 1st Lt. Robert B. Krogstad.

[8] A French Air Service term (in Italian, Brevetto) to indicate that a candidate had completed a prescribed course of instruction and was a designated military pilot.

Military Aviator), at which time our commissions are issued. While this will be my first Christmas away from home
and would love to be with you all, I shall at least enjoy
seeing Mt. Vesuvius, as well as getting a hot bath and a
change of underwear. Am going to get a camera and take
lots of pictures; will never forgive myself for not having
had one in France. Can't send any pictures home, but will
bring back some good ones. We read of the Halifax
disaster[9] in the New York *Herald* (Paris edition). It was
certainly awful and just remember we were in that same
harbor for three days and our ship also carried munitions.
A thing like that is worse than twice that number being
killed in battle.

[9]On December 6, 1917, half of Halifax, Nova Scotia, was destroyed
when the Norwegian vessel *Imo* collided with a French ship, the *Mont
Blanc*, laden with 5,000 tons of explosives. The explosion killed more
than 1,600 persons, injured 8,000 and destroyed 3,000 dwellings. Two
thousand more persons were listed as missing.

Campo d'Aviazione, Sud
Foggia, Italy
January 3, 1918

New Year's greetings and may it bring happiness, prosperity and peace to each of you.

My first Christmas away from home was full of thrills and wonderful sensations, but none supersede the longing in my heart to be at home among loved ones and to share with them the festivities of the season. I just feel as if I had missed a Christmas, as there was absolutely nothing about it here to remind one that such an occasion was at hand. We had three days holiday, which was spent by some in Rome, by others in Naples, I being with the latter contingent. Naples is about 80 miles from here, but it took us 11 hours to get there, so you can imagine what a joy it is to travel by train in Italy. It was very cold going across the mountains, but at Naples it was like summer. The first thing we did was to spend several hours in a hot bath, the first (but one) we have had since we left Paris. We had to argue with the proprietor for a long time before he would let us have any hot water: said he couldn't get any coal or wood at any price, but when we said we would go to another hotel he found that he did have some after all. We spent the rest of the day shopping. Next day we rode all over the city and visited Mt. Vesuvius (about 5 miles). It looks ominous enough from the city, but as we approached it appeared even more threatening. A little column of smoke could be seen rising from the crater and, of course, we thought that a violent eruption was imminent. When we got about half way up to the crater we ceased to wonder why Naples was so warm. No: we didn't get all the way up to the crater.

The next day we went to Pompeii—the most wonderful sight I ever saw. One cannot possibly realize without seeing it what an extraordinary place it is. It seemed as if the veil of the past had been lifted and we were allowed a vision of ancient history. The city is in a remarkable state of preservation and except for the missing roofs and broken columns on the public buildings and, of course, the absence of any inhabitants, it is just as it might have been 2,000 years ago. The amphitheatre and public baths are in almost perfect condition. In some of the houses they have the petrified bodies of entire families just as they were when caught by the molten lava from Vesuvius. I can't describe the sensations which I felt on walking through this ancient city, but it seemed as if time had turned backward and I was living in a long past age. In the museum at Naples they have the statues and works of art which were recovered from the ruins—magnificent specimens which to this day have not been equaled. That night we went to the opera *Andrew Shinea,* which was a new one on me, but the music was splendid. Of course all the words were in Italian, but music is a language in itself, which belongs to no single nation. Just think of grand opera—best seats— for 5 lire ($1, at present rate of exchange 60 cents). I wish Foggia was large enough to justify opera. Besides the sights we enjoyed fully as much the hot water and a chance to get something to eat besides the everlasting spaghetti. We also saw some magnificent cathedrals, with the most wonderful mural decorations. I failed to mention the most conspicuous thing about Naples—the army of so-called guides, who are really nothing but professional grafters, which has developed on account of so many tourists. They are the most persistent bunch I ever saw and have more different ways of separating money from an unsuspecting boob, with more money than brains, than the waiters in New York. But, as in every case except on the battle front, Uncle Sam's uniform was a great protection to us.

Returning to camp, we found that our baggage had arrived after spending six weeks around France and Italy, and it was good to have plenty of clothes, etc. again. The holiday baggage, mail and a consignment of oil stoves for the barracks made the season a very pleasant one, but according to my idea of a regular Christmas this might just as well have been General Lee's birthday. With the oil stoves came a return of our usual warm weather.

A Dr. Miller, former dean of the University of Missouri, has established a Y.M.C.A. which fills a big gap in the social life at the camp.

We have been making great progress in flying since Christmas. After a couple of rainy days the weather has been perfect and I have been getting a flight every day. It's the most wonderful sport in the world and the fellows will do anything to get a flight. A bad day calls forth some awful hard words that wouldn't pass in the Y.M.C.A.

Speaking of meeting people, I went to ground school with Monroe Good,[1] but never got to know him well until lately. We are on the same firing line. He is an all-American tackle from Colgate, knows Harold Carpenter very well and speaks highly of him. Also he had been negotiating to coach football at V.P.I. last year. He is a peach of a fellow even if he does come from Missouri.

I hope the censor will be good to me this time. I have always tried to be very careful, but that doesn't seem to

[1] 2nd Lt. Monroe Good.

make any difference; it all depends on how the censor feels when he attacks a letter.

Read two copies of *The Star* today—November 21 and 23.

Josiah P. Rowe, Jr.

Aviation Detachment
American Expeditionary Forces
Italy
January 14, 1918

Dearest Mother:

Referring to the cold weather, I don't see how the poor peasants have lived through this winter. In all Italy I haven't seen as many as fifty trees except those in the orchards and some small groves on the mountains.

In town it is a common sight to see whole families hovering over a little pan in which a few embers of charcoal are smoldering. It is more common to see a whole family without any means of heat at all. Fortunately, the cold weather didn't last very long and a few oil stoves from Rome kept us from freezing. Unless one has been here it is impossible to imagine the extent of poverty which exists—there is nothing in the United States like it—and in every city there is a regular army of beggars. The Italian soldiers are paid ten centissimi (2 cents) a day and for meals get a few spoonfuls of unseasoned spaghetti and a piece of hard brown bread.

Since flying is the principal thing I do these days, you might like to know what it is like. After bundling up in a heavy sheepskin coat, helmet, goggles and gloves, you get in the machine and strap yourself to the seat. Then test the controls—rudder, aileron and elevator—to see if they are all right, then start the motor. They can't use mufflers on the engines, as it reduces the power, and the noise is almost deafening, but you get accustomed to it. The plane starts off slowly, gradually gaining speed until you are going about 90 miles an hour—pretty fast. Unless you use the elevator you can't tell when you leave the ground and when you look over the side of the body the earth appears to have dropped away, and is still falling. When you get up about 500 metres (1,500 ft.) a person on the ground is just a speck and the country is like a big checkerboard with fields of green and brown as the squares. Then you turn and in doing so have to bank the machine, and if you look down you will see that someone has twisted the earth around sideways. Then you turn the other way and the earth has moved in the other direction, but when the plane is straightened out the old world gets level again.

It seems funny to see the earth wobbling around so— first just below your left wing, then right under the other wing. You can see for miles and miles around, a whole train looks like it is about an inch long. Some of the fellows on the altitude tests say they have seen both the Adriatic and Mediterranean seas at the same time. While you are going along about 90 miles an hour you are hardly aware of any motion at all except for the wind, which is driving against your face. You see a little village away off in front of you and soon you are right over it, but you hardly realize during this time that you are getting any closer to it, because you have nothing by which to judge your speed as you have in an automobile or train. Then you shut off your motor and glide towards camp, or rather the earth begins to rise towards you until it touches the wheels and the plane rolls along until it stops. All the way down you have a funny feeling in your ears and when you get to the ground your head feels all stopped up and you can't hear very well. This is caused by the difference of the air pressure on the ground and up in the air. You don't notice this in ascending as you go up so gradually.

This is great sheep-raising country around Foggia and sometimes when a student is flying and sees a flock of sheep with several boys minding them he will drive straight towards them until within 15 or 20 feet and then go up again. The boys get more frightened than the sheep, but they all do their best to get out of the way and it is funny to see them scatter so.

In Italy

Campo d'Aviazione, Sud
Foggia, Italy
January 22, 1918

A new detachment arrived several days ago from France and the West Camp is now in operation. (This is the South Camp.) The West Camp is about 2½ miles from here and as soon as we got a chance we walked over to see if there was anyone we knew in the crowd. Many of the boys found old-time friends, but there were none whom I knew except one fellow who was in my battery at Fort Myer—Woodworth[1]—from New Jersey. You remember that I wrote you about my second week at Princeton, telling of a squadron that was sent off on just a few hours' notice. Well, in this last detachment we found many of those same fellows. They sailed about September 20 and have since been in a French camp doing guard duty, cooking, ditch digging, etc., almost everything except flying. They have been leading a hard life and say that Italy looks like Paradise to them. It was just by the merest chance that we were sent here instead of spending a few months in a French camp. As we found out afterwards there was a detachment of students on another ship in our convoy which was destined to come to Italy as per Washington orders, but just because we docked first in Liverpool and consequently reached Paris first, our detachment got the orders intended for our belated comrades, who are now enjoying a miserable existence in France, which would have been ours except for blind chance.

The weather has been ideal for the past two weeks and we have been making fine progress with our flying. My

[1] 1st Lt. Earl C. Woodworth.

instructor, Pezolli, is very slow and will not let a man go until he is confident of his ability to handle a plane alone. Even on a perfect day he will not give anyone more than one lesson, whereas others give as many as possible in order to speed things up. I don't mind the delay, as one never learns too much before taking his initial flight alone, and none of Pezolli's pupils has ever had a smashup. Still I expect to be soloing in a week and then I will be able to take some aerial pictures to send you.

I believe I mentioned something about a little hostility toward us on the part of the townspeople, but this has entirely disappeared and a warm attachment has sprung up in its place. This is due in part to a growing realization that America is in earnest about the war and that her forces are going to win it, although I would not express it to them that way. We have to convey the idea that we consider it an honor to be permitted to help them. But the reversion of feeling is more due to the fortunes that the stores and restaurants are making out of us. Foggia has become so inflated with prosperity that it will be years before they regain their normal state. I saw a handsome meerschaum pipe the other night priced at 30 lire. I bargained the old woman down to 20. The next night I started where I left off and got her down to 12 and then bought it. An Italian could have gotten it for about 6 or 7. They have two sets of prices and no matter if a store is full of Italians and a single American comes in he gets the undivided attention of the clerks. We are getting to be expert with the language and can now order two fried eggs without having to make signs and crow like a chicken. With the exception of a few simple words, our ability to converse with the people consists of adding an "o" or an "a" to the English words and changing the accent a little. It is remarkable how well one can get along this way. The language is really pretty and

it is a regular picnic to hear them rave. They don't talk—
they sing—and they do it so fast that it is practically
unintelligible, but the effect is highly pleasing to the ear.
They put so much emphasis into everything they say that
unless you catch a few stray words of a conversation you
can't tell whether they are inquiring after each other's
health or having a family row over their children.

The main fault I find with Italy—besides the
spaghetti—is the feminine sex. I haven't found the romantic atmosphere that the story books lead one to expect and
the "Bella Fouchullas" are not so "Bella" as one would
imagine. Most of them have beautiful black hair and eyes,
but in every other respect they are hopeless. The chief
trouble is their dress—they seem to dress just because the
law requires it, but what they wear or how it looks never
causes them any sleepless nights. I guess some parents I
know wish that their children had this trait. Perhaps if we
hadn't seen the French girls first, the Italians would have
made a better impression, but after Paris they are quite
"impossible."

Thanks to the Y.M.C.A., matters are gradually im-
proving and soon we expect to have a library in which to
spend our spare hours. We have quite a nice little room
now with magazines, a piano, and a phonograph, which
serve to enliven the time.

Thanks to Taylor and Julia Mason for their liberal sub-
scriptions to the Army Y.M.C.A. They certainly do a wonderful work in keeping the spirits and morals of the men
from going to the bad.

I haven't received the box yet, but it is coming and I
can almost taste that good fruit cake and candy. Christmas
packages are still coming in, although sent early in November, and mine may come at any time.

In France the women do practically everything—they

run the trains, street cars, motor trucks, barbershops, and saloons. The same is partially true of England and Italy. There are more women and girls over here than there are in Taylor's mind.

In speaking of the Italians, there is one thing I failed to mention. If there is anything they like better than having their picture taken, which gives them the utmost pleasure, it is music. They are musical to the last degree and the majority of them know all about opera. Out on the flying line if one of us begins to whistle a strain from any opera the "motoriste" takes it right up and carries it beyond the point where my memory fails me. The people on the street, the cab drivers and soldiers go along singing—not "What Do You Want to Make Those Eyes at Me For" or "There's a Little Bit of Bad in Every Good Little Girl," but *Il Trovatore, Carmen, Faust,* etc.

The principal reason I go into town as often as I do is because at one of the cafes an old man and woman playing a mandolin and guitar play more classical music in one night than I would know in a life time. Whenever we want a selection played, but can't tell them the name, we just hum a line and they go right ahead and play the whole thing through and in many cases the Italians will join in and sing. There are many budding Carusos here and they like to demonstrate their talent. We enjoy it more than they do.

Tell Papa we didn't forget General Lee's birthday. The Dixie boys started to declare a holiday, but the flying promised more amusement. It is very warm now, sometimes hot, and we are beginning to shed the heavies. Have read in *The Star* of the severe cold at home and I sympathize with the Fredericksburg folks.

In Italy

Campo d'Aviazione, Sud
Foggia, Italy
January 28, 1918

I have just received your letter of December 16. I see Maurice[1] and Reginald have joined the Aviation Corps. The aviation service offers many advantages over other arms and the aviator receives every consideration. That much alone sounds selfish and might be misinterpreted to mean that a man who goes in for aviation is picking out a soft job, but you must remember that the aviator is in a position to render more valuable service than a whole regiment of men. In fact, there may be times when the whole regiment may thank their stars that the "eyes of the army" are on the job. The doughboys may claim that aviation is a lazy man's game, but just because we don't have to dig trenches, clean guns and stand guard duty is no sign that we do not have anything to do.

An aviator has to be a wireless wizard, able to send and receive 8 to 10 words a minute; a machine gun expert, able to take down and assemble the entire mechanism in one minute, also be able to do it in the dark; he must have a wide theoretical and practical knowledge of motors, must know all about the design and construction of aeroplanes, must know enough about astronomy to steer a course by the stars, must be able to handle a plane under all conditions and, finally, must be a better flyer than the Hun.

I am glad Reg has enlisted and I only wish that we could get together. The military training will do worlds for him and he will have some wonderful experiences. His hardest work will be at ground school and he will have to

[1]Maurice B. Rowe, a first cousin from Fredericksburg.

put all he has into it. Those two months were the hardest I ever went through, but I am confident that he can do the work. In all probability he will take his flying training in the United States as all the schools over here are full, but there may be vacancies by the time he finishes ground school. His absence makes a deep gap in the home circle, but it won't be for long and we will appreciate each other all the more when we are reunited. Home isn't what it used to be with all the children gone except Taylor and Julia Mason, but it won't be long before the house will be resounding with the old-time laughter as of childhood. Although most of us have passed that happy period and the innocent pleasures of childhood will not come again, one can never grow so old as not to feel the spell of youthful joys and we will all be kids again when we get back together. That sounds like I am a million years old, doesn't it?

We flew this morning for the first time in four days on account of the wind and a fellow certainly gets rusty when he misses so much time. I made some landings that would make a beginner ashamed, bouncing about 40 feet, but fortunately didn't break anything.

I am sending a few snapshots which I hope the censor will be kind enough to pass. Am also numbering this letter and will continue to do so, so that you will know when any are lost. You do likewise.

The order has just come down from Paris that the old "service hat" has been relegated to the junk pile, being supplanted by a cocky little hat something like the Royal Flying Corps. This ruling applies only to troops on this side. We haven't seen the new lid yet, but regardless of what it looks like we will hate to give up this distinctive American feature. There is something about an American soldier, some personal distinction, which readily differentiates him from others, but the old service hat was the one outstanding and unmistakable feature which proclaimed an American at all times and amid all surroundings.

The Australian troops wear service hats also, but the brim is turned up on one side. Somehow, a service hat, though tattered and torn and bent and mis-shapen, seems to make a fellow look more manly, probably because it is associated with the West, and they will have to go a long way to find a hat more satisfactory.

Haven't received the box yet, but I have an intimation that it is coming tomorrow. Have been having the same hope every day for a month.

Campo d'Aviazione, Sud
Foggia, Italy
February 16, 1918

A most exciting event happened several days ago—I took my first "solo" flight! There really wasn't anything exciting about it—except me. Before going up, my feelings were many and varied—I was eager to make the flight without an instructor in front who invariably makes you go to the right when you want to go to the left and says to go down when you want to go up, but still the instructor's presence, while aggravating at times, always inspired a feeling of confidence which was strangely lacking when I climbed into the machine alone. I confess that I was nervous and I don't know which vibrated the more, the engine or my knees. As I opened up the motor and began taxiing along the ground a thousand possibilities entered my mind, but I put them all aside and resigned myself with the thought: "Well, I'm off and it's a make or a break." But as soon as I left the ground I forgot all my fears, as there was so much else to think of. I knew the instructor was observing me, so I began to think "Am I climbing too fast? Am I climbing fast enough? Am I going straight?" After getting to 200 metres, I experienced a feeling of absolute power and freedom—the whole air and heavens were my playground and I had to fight against the desire to see just what tricks the machine was capable of doing. I was tempted to set out for America to get a taste of something besides spaghetti and to see a girl who had any kind of hair and eyes except black and who knew the art of wearing clothes, but then I struck a "Bump," or rather it struck me, and I decided that it was better to see if I could complete the tour of the camp before venturing on any long voyages. Then with my eyes glued on the tachometer (rev. per minute of nestor), gas pressure gauge, oil pressure gauge, and altimeter, (thank heavens that at this stage we don't need a compass, maps, drift meter and buoyancy meter), and looking ahead, behind, overhead, underneath, to the right and left for other machines, and watching the ground for indications of the course, you can see that I didn't have time to twirl my thumbs and I didn't give much thought to the developments of the Russian Revolution or the merits of nationwide prohibition. I was looking everywhere at once, but didn't see a whole lot and from observations on that flight alone I couldn't tell you whether the earth appeared green or pink. Eventually I got around the course, shut off the motor and glided down to the landing ground. I heaved a sigh of relief when I felt my wheels— no, the wheels of the machine—running along the ground. When the plane stopped and I got out I thought surely I had been gone for an hour and a half, but the official figures showed that I went up at 13:56 and came down at 14:00 o'clock. (That's the way they count time over here.) Upon thinking over the incidents of my flight I concluded that the instructor had been only kidding me when he had said "Multo Bene" and "Benissimes" after various lessons and that I wasn't quite such a good aviator as I had fancied myself. Now maybe I will really begin to learn something.

On my second solo flight I felt perfectly at ease, really more so in the air than on the ground because as long as one remains in the air he is perfectly safe—it is only when you strike the ground that you are liable to be jarred. With each succeeding flight now I feel more confidence and I hate to get out of the machine even more than I hate to get out of bed in the mornings.

"Bumps" in the air, as mentioned above, are very uncertain and irritating, because you can't see them and you don't know they are there until you strike them. They are caused by "convection currents" of air, that is, the radiation of heat from the earth. The sun heats up the ground, and the ground heats up the air, and the air like a human being who is "all het up" acts queerly. If all the earth were exactly alike there wouldn't be any "bumps," but a green field gives off less heat than a plowed field; sometimes one part of a field will give off more heat than another part of the same field; a building in a field doesn't give off the same amount of heat as the earth around it; the exposed side of a hill radiates more heat than the shady side; and so the air is full of varying air currents to which the aeroplane is minutely sensitive. You can always tell when you cross a road without even looking down on it. While you cannot see a "bump" you can always tell when you hit one—you either go up or down or you are tipped over on one side. On a very hot day the "bumps" are more noticeable and are sometimes dangerous. Many a day when the sun is shining brightly and not a whiff of air is stirring we don't fly because it is "too much bumpy."

Some time ago one of the students while on his cross-country flight got lost in a cloud, missed his course, and after flying aimlessly around for an hour or more trying to get his bearings he was forced to land in a rural district near Naples, 100 miles from camp. He came down in a farm yard and was quickly surrounded by a crowd of curious peasants. They had never seen an American, but knew that he was not Italian so concluded that he must be an Austrian. Armed with sticks and pitchforks and a mistaken idea, they were about to make him a prisoner, when one arrived who could speak English. When they were convinced that he was an American and was not bent on blowing up their homes they "fell on his neck" and tried to outdo each other in showing him every attention. The general of that district came out and took the fellow to his home in Naples, where he was dined and feasted like a king. Believe me, the best thing that can happen to a fellow these days is to be an American.

Yesterday I received a nice letter from the Rev. D. G. Whittinghill, Baptist missionary in Rome, saying that he had learned through you that I was in Foggia; that he was coming through this section shortly and expected to stop off here to see me and the other Baptist boys in camp. His letter was very cordial and I hope he can come down here, and I shall also make it a point to call on him when I am in Rome. Isn't it strange that no matter where you go you invariably find some one you know either directly or indirectly. He informed me that his wife's mother was a Miss Braxton, having been born and reared in Fredericksburg, and was married at "Hazel Hill." I shall be glad to meet them for personal as well as religious reasons. It was very kind of you to write to him and I appreciate it highly. Except for you, I am afraid us Baptists here would not have received any spiritual attention. It may interest you to know that Catholic priests have been here several times to administer communion and hold mass. I have some very interesting facts to tell you about the spiritual attitude of the men here, but I will not go into it now, except to say that all are college men and of a very high type and their morals are above reproach. Aside from their religious beliefs, and while not renouncing them in the least, there is a growing sentiment of fatalism for the time being. The men are taking chances and preparing to take greater ones and they can't help feeling that if anything is going to happen to them it is all predestined and that it is entirely beyond their power to prevent or change the operations of the inevitable. This is really the only way in which a fellow can keep his nerve. "There is a fate which shapes our ends, rough-hew them how we will."

In Italy

Campo d'Aviazione, Sud
Foggia, Italy
March 2, 1918

I can't help from smiling in sweet satisfaction and smacking my lips with ecstatic bliss at every thought of the rapturous hours spent in riotous living immediately after the receipt of the long-looked-for box on Saturday, February 24. Such tasty morsels of such delicate food have never caused more genuine joy and happiness in the heart (?) of man before. Mother dear, I can never thank you and the others in proportion with what you deserve for sending me such a nice, large box of so many good things, but let it be known that I deeply appreciate it all not only for the thoughtfulness which it represented, but also because of the aching void which was filled and the pangs of hunger which were appeased. The box had been on the way for such a long time and I had daily expected it for so many disappointing weeks that I had really given it up for lost, but the delay only served to increase the joy of receiving and consuming its contents. I thank you very much for the wonderful fruit cake and jam, and for the chocolate, mints, gum and writing paper, and _____ for their liberal contributions of figs, dates and chocolate. I can't thank them for anything specific, as I was out on the flying field when the box arrived, so that when I came in the feast was spread and their cards had been removed. I shared the things with some other boys in return for some bits from their boxes, but believe me I defended that fruit cake with my life and stretched it out over two days of blissful contentment. The box, although having been three months in transit, was in perfect condition and the contents were in no way impaired by the long delay. Again I thank you all most sincerely for all the dainty delicacies that so delighted me and others. As "interior decorators" you are incomparable.

I know it is sacrilegious to mention spaghetti in the same breath with such rare things as the box contained, but while on the subject of food I want to tell you that lately our mess has improved beyond the most sanguine expectations. Just when our hunger was becoming unbearable and we were getting desperate for want of real food, along came the good old beans and rescued us from the misery of hunger and famine. It seems impossible to maintain an army without beans; they are as essential to the men as powder is to the guns. The old army mainstay has been the object of many a vigorous and impassioned malediction, but we welcomed the beans with unfeigned delight and a hearty relish. Instead of macaroni every day we now have frequent dishes of beans and we are no longer wasting away for want of nourishment. The beans were doubly welcome because just a short time before their arrival, an order was issued forbidding us to eat or drink anything in the city of Foggia on account of the awful sanitary conditions. The order was quite necessary from a medical standpoint, but it was a distinct shock to our appetites, as we could no longer go to town to get fried eggs and something that looked like beefsteak, which had been an agreeable diversion from the endless monotony of spaghetti, even though everything was fried in olive oil instead of lard or ham grease. But just in the nick of time, when we were contemplating a raid on all nearby pastures to offset the effects of slow starvation, a divine providence or else a good mess sergeant sent us the beans. You may be interested and surprised to know that I am taking on weight rapidly without the slightest regard for the limits of stretchability of my clothes and I can now boast of the enormous bulk of 66 kilograms (145 lbs.). You wouldn't think that spaghetti, bitter oranges and figs could do so much for me, would you? I wouldn't either if all the scales I have tried didn't register the same figures.

In addition to the box, I have received two packages of knitted goods from two very sweet and lovable maidens, one of them being the charming Miss Winifred Shelly (New York) who, by the way, can knit quite as well as she can paint pretty pictures and entertain a backward cousin from the country. The thoughtfulness and painstaking effort of these two adorable girls was highly appreciated and I shall prize these samples of their handiwork far more than they dared to hope. I might say that fate, and the girls, have been very generous with the knitted goods and I now have enough sweaters, helmets, scarves and wristlets to start a store or a quartermaster's supply depot, although the demand for such articles is not very great now, since the sun is working overtime in the effort to redeem itself for its neglect a few weeks ago. The thermometer is beginning to hit the high places now and we have discarded the X, Y, Z's in favor of the B.V.D.'s.

Flying is going along nicely and the air is full of planes and the hum of motors all day long. I am making good headway with my "solo" work, climbs, glides, banks and turns. Nearly everyone who writes to me (and there aren't many) seems to think it is their duty to caution me against going too high. I appreciate their interest, but they are all wrong about the altitude. Contrary to the rules and principles of life, in aviation the "high flier" is the safest. So far I have been up to 1,200 metres, but even from that height if my motor should go bad, I could glide for three miles before landing, and this feature of flying has saved many a plane from wreckage and the pilot from spending the night in an open field or in the squatty, dirty little house of a peasant. I have been "soloing" for about three weeks, but was interrupted by a spell of bad weather. Am at it again now and with every ride I gain new confidence and no longer does my heart go up in my mouth every time my plane goes up in the air. Flying is certainly a great, invigorating sport—no matter how glum or dumpy one feels, as soon as the motor starts its roaring and the plane rises off the ground he forgets the blues and takes a new interest in life. It is well that it is thus because if a person is not concerned with life when up in the air there is apt to be one less life when he comes down. Don't interpret this to mean that flying is dangerous, as anything may be dangerous if a person goes to sleep on the job. Just about a week ago, one of the men who had finished his Brevet without the slightest mishap had his shoulder badly wrenched and was bruised up in general by falling off a motor truck.

It grieves me sorely to see that General Pershing[1] is not over-flowing with affection for the aviators, although he is depending on them to win the war. Upon enlisting, and while at ground school, we were given the rosiest promises of first lieutenant commissions, but General Pershing has overruled this and substituted seconds, which most of us have gotten at training camp. In addition, he has recommended to Washington that 25 percent flying pay for officers be discontinued. If this is adopted it will be an official recognition that aviation is not as dangerous as formerly, but I would rather have the extra 25 percent than the official recognition. But we would rather get a couple

[1]General John J. Pershing, commander of the American Expeditionary Force (AEF), which consisted of all American military personnel who served in Europe during World War I.

of Huns than a couple of shoulder bars anyhow. Shoulder bars and a Sam Browne belt[2] make a man look better, but they don't make him fly any better, and I would rather be a good aviator and a private all my life than be a poor flier and have all the decorations that belong to an officer. Of course, a commission is not to be despised and at home it makes a great difference, but over here it is entirely a secondary consideration. We are bound to get a commission when we finish our second Brevet, but we are more concerned about making "vaseline landings" and straight lines on the barograph than we are about making an appointment with the photographer as soon as we get on our duds. I have gotten so now I don't give a hang about a lieutenancy (maybe if I wasn't so sure of getting one I wouldn't feel this way), but I certainly would like to get through with my training and get up to the front in time to help knock the stuffings out of the Germans.

Our Y.M.C.A. has taken a hump on itself lately and is now the most popular place in camp. We used to go over frequently to get warm and pick up a handful of stationery, but now everyone takes an active interest in it. A new director came down from France recently and he succeeded in smuggling over a shipment of baseballs, bats, gloves, etc. that we have been trying to get ever since we came down here, but which the Italian customs officers would not pass, as they were considered as childish and uscless toys. We have fixed up a diamond and play every afternoon. Soon we will be having regular games with the boys at the West Camp and thus profitably spend the time on nonflying days as well as get some greatly needed exercise. It may get too windy for flying, but never too rough

[2]A wide leather belt with a narrow strap going across the body and over the right shoulder that supported the belt on the pistol side. Worn by most officers overseas during World War I.

for a baseball game. The Italians try to play, but they don't know a thing about it and I am afraid they never will; they are so backward about it. You know, about a week ago I saw a group of children playing some kind of game that looked like "Ring Around the Roses", and this was the first time since I had been in Italy that I had seen children playing. I think this is the secret of many of Italy's faults; the children don't know how to play. Therein lies the reason for the weak, sickly looking children, the sallow complexions, the dull faces, the stunted, almost dwarfish growth, and the universal indolence of the people. The kids smoke from the time they discard dresses for breeches and they have no conception of sport, the only game I ever saw them playing being that of pitching and matching pennies. They don't know the joys of Tag, Hiding, Run, Sheep, Run, Puss in the Corner, and such healthy innocent games of childhood, and they don't know what fun it is to steal off from home and go swimming when they should be cutting the grass, and they have never experienced the supreme thrills of sliding to second, or tagging a runner out at third, or knocking a home run, etc., when they ought to be pulling up weeds in the garden. Do you wonder that they are small of stature and weak physically? Another glaring fault is that the boys and young men don't go with girls; they live entirely apart from each other, the girls staying home and minding the babies (and there are thousands of them—no family is complete without two or three dirty little tots) or washing clothes while the boys are around the streets pitching pennies and collecting cigarette butts. You never see a boy and girl together on the streets or even husband and wife for that matter. The boys ignore the girls entirely until they reach a certain age and then they seem to get married purely as a business proposition. They don't know the joys (and sorrows) of a childhood flirtation, to feel the heart beat madly and the face blush hotly in answer to a sweetheart's smiles; to become dizzy with delight at the warm touch of "her" hand, and to try to write poetry in "her" name and honor. How can the manhood of any nation be all it is capable of without the refining and elevating influences of womanhood?

But to get back to the Y.M.C.A. You would hardly think that Albert Spaulding, the great American violinist, and Lt. Spaulding, U.S. Air Service, were one and the same, but they most certainly are. He came down from France some time ago to get his flying training and happily he brought his violin with him. He has given some wonderful concerts in the Y.M.C.A. and I never heard such great music in my life. He is truly a marvel and if he flies as well as he plays, the Germans will regret their part in teaching such a masterful musician. He gave a concert in the Teatro Duano in town for the benefit of the refugees from the neighborhood of Venice and the Italians went wild over him—"Vive Americano, Vive Signor Spaulding-a." Just as a novelty which we thought the Italians would appreciate, or at least be amused by, the "Jazz Band" from camp, consisting of guitars, banjos, violins, ukeleles, mandolins and a drum, played several real raggy numbers like "Oh, Johnny," "On the Beach at Waikiki," "Yaacka Hicky Doola," etc., that would go fine in the States, but that night it was miserably flat. The boys put all kinds of "pep" into it, but the Italians did not like it at all; they didn't know what to make of it.

I wish there wasn't any censorship; there are so many things I would like to tell you, but I am afraid the scissors might be too near at hand when the censor reads them. He may be cutting up or even destroying my letters already, but if he is I will never speak to him again. If you fail to get any letters or if he cuts out anything you must be sure and let me know what it was. I hope you received the pictures I sent, but I wouldn't be surprised if they were removed. I am taking a chance that the censor has just received a sweet letter from his girl and that while rejoicing over his good fortune he will let the enclosed pictures (6) get by. The pictures are only fairly good, due to the poor work in developing them. Among many other things that they can't do over here, developing and printing pictures is a conspicuous item. I also enclose a poem, which I received shortly from John H. Small, Jr., of Washington, a son of Congressman Small, of North Carolina, a nephew or cousin or something of Secretary Daniels. He was in my battery at Fort Myer, also with me in ground school at Princeton. He is now taking his flying training in Texas and apparently finds time to write good poetry. I also enclose a newspaper clipping of a poem which contains a mixture of humor and satire, which appealed to me immensely. Not to be knocking the draft or the attending festivities, but the fellows who volunteered seem to have been forgotten in all the hurrah, spread-eagle stuff connected with the draft.

I haven't had any letters from home since my last letter, but we are about due for a big bunch of mail and I am expecting letters. I have sent several magazines home and I hope you got them all right. I believe I told you that Aunt Nellie[3] is sending me the *New York Times* which I get regularly and with The Fredericksburg *Star* I am now getting the two best papers in the world and manage to keep posted on what happens in the States.

I am very anxious to know all about what Reg is doing, also the news from Mossie.[4] I notice from *The Star* that quite a number of the local boys have enlisted in the Avia-

[3]Mrs. Daniel Garber, a maternal aunt.
[4]Maurice B. Rowe, his cousin.

tion Corps; they couldn't pick anything better, and by joining the "highest" branch of the service they have shown a commendable desire to "elevate" themselves. It sure would be great to meet Reg when I get back to France, but I am afraid such an event is too much to hope for. One of the best friends I have is a capital fellow named Walker, from New Jersey, who was in my battery at Fort Myer. He went to ground school with me; we used to spend our weekends together, and were the best of chums. Why, we even had the same girl in Trenton, but when I left ground school, I left him (and the girl, too) and I don't expect to see him again until after the war, probably at some Grand Reunion of Veterans of the Great War about thirty years from now. The same War Department that enlisted two men of the same qualifications from the same organization into the same branch of the service at the same time, sent them to the same ground school to pursue the same studies with the same degree of success and then sent one to Louisiana and the other to Italy will certainly see to it that two brothers shall not by any chance meet up with each other in France.

Best love to all the family, friends, neighbors, relatives and Normalites,[5] and "mille grazie" for the box.

Devotedly,

Josiah P. Rowe, Jr.

[5]Students at the State Normal School.

Campo d'Aviazione, Sud
Foggia, Italy
March 8, 1918

Our camp is about one and one-half miles from Foggia, in the "ankle" of Italy, 80 miles from Naples and 120 miles from Rome, and is situated on a perfectly flat area of about fifty square miles between two mountain ranges. This region is the scene of Hannibal's great campaign in which he used his army of elephants and no one knows how many of the old Roman battles were fought over the same ground. There is a cathedral in town now in use which was built in the year 650 (A.D. or B.C. I don't know which) and I don't think they have ever removed a particle of dirt since that time. Foggia is a city of about 40,000 people and is what I would call a third class Italian city. The place is built entirely of stone houses, sidewalks and streets. I haven't seen a frame building in all Italy. Wood is the scarcest kind of a thing over here—the wood we burn in the Y.M.C.A. is not bought by the cord or wagon load, but by the kilogram (2 lbs.). Foggia doesn't cover an inch more area than Fredericksburg, so you can imagine that their parks and front yards aren't very large. The worst thing about the town is the fact that there isn't a drop of running water in the whole place—I know it sounds strange, but it is true nevertheless. There are two municipal wells from which the water is drawn in small kegs and is then distributed to the homes in small donkey carts. The people cannot afford to use much water when the total supply for a whole family for all purposes is two kegs. They have no sewers, although they try to use the streets as a substitute, which wouldn't be so bad if the city were not perfectly flat. In the afternoons, the nearby farmers bring their dairies and young dairies, consisting of cows and goats, into town; drive them right up to the customer's door and draw the milk right into the family pitcher. This used to seem awfully strange to us, but now we think nothing of kicking a goat or pushing an old brindle cow out of the way. You can get an idea of the unspeakable sanitary conditions from the fact that our medical authorities have prohibited us from eating or drinking anything in the town. The only excuse I know of for Foggia is that it is the center of a great sheep raising section, and that the Italian trains have to stop every two or three miles whether there is a station or not and the stations on either side of us are about six miles distant, so Foggia just happened.

Our camp is an excellent one—without a doubt the best in Europe. We are quartered in large, stone barracks, have real beds with real springs, running water, electric lights, and every reasonable convenience. Our mess hall is fine, for army life, and we have a waiter for every twelve men. These waiters are all Italian soldiers, who have been wounded at the front, and they are so anxious to stay here and not be sent back into the fighting that they overdo themselves in their desire to please us. In spite of our comfortable surroundings, the men are not satisfied and would not be if this were Paradise itself, because this is not France; it is not the front and it is not like war. We didn't come over here to get a soft bed, but rather to get a Hun. The one big question that is asked a hundred times a day is, "When will we get back home?" Next to that is "When will we get some mail?"

We get up in the morning to the hum of a hundred motors, fly all day long, and go to bed hoping for good weather on the morrow. The air is full of planes from morn 'til night—on one side of the field are the S.I.A.'s, small, fast and handsome; in the center are the mammoth Capronis, which, with their three high-powered motors, sound like a thousand machine guns in action and look like an apartment house; on the other side are the Farman training planes, in which the students are learning the principles of flying. The Americans are always eager to fly and the machines are never idle except when the weather man gets peeved and hands out rain and wind. The Italians are naturally high strung and easily excitable and the stunts which the Americans do don't help in the least to make them more rational and less demonstrative. Every time two planes get within a hundred metres of each other they wave their arms frantically and yell like demons, and when a student looks as if he will surely crash into a building, they tear their hair and jump around distractedly. The Italian students will never do any fancy stunts because they say that the Americans will go right up and try something twice as hard and will certainly get hurt. When we start the acrobatic school I know some of the Italians are going plumb crazy. We have had some hairbreadth escapes and many minor accidents, but so far none of the students has been seriously hurt. The instructors say that we are "very much lucky" and that we will surely win the war, as the Germans will never be able to kill us.

The country around here is awfully dry and unattractive, but from the air it looks beautiful, the colors being greatly accentuated. Green looks like green and a plowed field shows up in the richest brown. The little villages look like silver lakes and the roads like strips of white ribbon. A real estate agent would never have any trouble selling a farm if he would give his prospective customer a look at it from an aeroplane. From a height of 1,000 metres it is possible to see the Adriatic Sea, and from 2,000 both the

Adriatic and the Mediterranean can be seen. I am going up about 5,000 metres some day and take a squint at Fredericksburg, but no matter how high I go I can't see why someone doesn't write to me.

I am getting along nicely with my flying and in about six more flights I will be through my 1st Brevet. When I finish my 2nd Brevet (if I do) I will receive the Italian Eagle, membership to the Aero Club of Italy, the U.S. Reserve Military Aviator Insignia, a lieutenant's commission, a three days' leave to Rome, and what I hope for above all else, a chance to get up to the front and help blind the eyes of Germany.

I have enjoyed the time spent here, although I wish that our camp could have been situated near some other city, and really I like Italy very well. About a third of the men one meets have been to America working in the mines of Pennsylvania, the steel mills of Ohio or the subways of New York and it is funny to be walking along the street and hear someone say "Hello Keed." As soon as the war is over all these people and many more are going to America on the first ship they can get. If one likes spaghetti and doesn't mind a little dirt they should be able to have a good time in Italy, provided they can stand the abominable train system and can eat eggs fried in olive oil.

I thank you again for sending me *The Star*. I have been away from home before for months, but never have I been separated from *The Star* for such a long time as I was before I received my first copy here.

Josiah P. Rowe, Jr.

Campo d'Aviazione, Sud
Foggia, Italy
March 13, 1918

I am leaving for Rome tonight and I must write now or else put it off a week or more and probably have what few items I have to mention crowded out by the sights and sensations of Rome. I was able to get leave as I finished my 1st Brevet yesterday and was entitled to either go now or wait until after my 2nd Brevet, but I think Rome will be more attractive now than after it begins to get hot and, besides, away back in the dark recesses of my brain there lurks an old time axiom about a "bird in the hand," etc. I am going with Tom Ewing,[1] of New York, formerly of Washington, a junior at Yale, whom I knew at ground school. Am going to see and do everything that is possible in three days and will write you all about it when I get back.

The words "1st Brevet" probably don't mean much to you, so I will tell you of a few of the things which it contains. To begin with, when a student finishes on the dual control machines, he is sent to the "Giro Line," where he does his first "solo" work, making four "Giro di Campos" at a height of 150 metres to get him used to handling the machine alone. Then he does four quarter-turns, climbing to 300 metres, cutting off the motor and gliding at right angles to the landing ground and at 100 metres, turning and landing straight. Then come four half-turns, cutting off at 300 metres directly over the landing ground and headed in the opposite direction to that of landing. Then he has to

[1]2nd Lt. Thomas R. Ewing, Jr., 13th Aero Squadron.

do two "Doppios," cutting off at 600 metres and gliding down to a figure eight. Next is the "Alinimento," climbing to 1,000 metres, cutting off and gliding down to 600, turning on the motor and doing figure eights at a constant altitude for fifteen minutes. Then come two sets of eights, practice and official, climbing to 600 metres. Finally he does the "Forty-five minutes," climbing 1,000 metres and remaining at that altitude for forty-five minutes.

Perhaps you will be disappointed that I am not doing "loops," spirals and spinning nose-dives, etc., but you see we have to go about this in a gradual manner. None of our 1st Brevet tests were bad after they had been done, but believe me on the half-turns and "Doppios" where you have to "bank" the plane up over sixty degrees and work your ailerons, rudder, and elevator at the same time, you get "some" sensation. On the figure eights and the 45-minute test, you use a barograph, which is very sensitive and records the slightest variation in altitude and it is very difficult to obtain a straight line, especially if it is a "bumpy" day. Some of the lines look like a cross-cut saw and mine was far from straight, but I didn't vary more than 25 metres. On the 45-minute ride I had a regular picnic. It takes about seven minutes to climb to 1,000 metres (with the training planes) and about three to glide down, so the whole flight lasts nearly an hour. The day was windy but smooth and I had a fine machine, so I had plenty of time to look around and enjoy the scenery. After reaching a thousand, I throttled the motor down so the plane would not tend to climb, and with one eye on the barograph needle and noting the various gauges and indicators I just sat there and gazed all over creation. This is interesting enough for a while, but in ten minutes I had seen everything from the Adriatic Sea to the mountains and I feared that time would hang heavy on my hands.

Campo d'Aviazione, Sud
Foggia, Italy
March 24, 1918

I haven't written sooner because I have been trying to assemble my thoughts so as to put the impressions of my wonderful trip to Rome in some kind of readable form, but after a week of thinking and reflecting, I am convinced that it is useless to attempt any assimilation of ideas as I would certainly end up in a hopeless jumble, so I shall describe in a spontaneous way the experiences of this visit to the ancient capital of the world.

I went with Tom Ewing, of whom I wrote you, and no small part of my enjoyment was due to his highly agreeable company. We left Foggia at 12 o'clock (called 24 o'clock over here) on the night of the 13th and arrived in Rome at 9 the next morning. We had sleepers, but we got up early, partly because we couldn't sleep and partly to look at the scenery which was very attractive. The country was quite hilly, but every inch of ground was under cultivation. Orchards and vineyards only stop when they reach the peasant's front door. You never see a fence of any kind over here and the long stretches of plains with alternate fields of green and brown and the foothills which were worked to the very summit made a picture that can be seen nowhere except in Italy. On some of the hilltops were little villages built entirely of stone, all jammed up together with scarcely breathing space, while there were miles and miles of room on every side, showing the influence of the tribal spirit of olden days. But I am supposed to be telling you of Rome.

Nearing the outskirts we saw the remains of the old aqueduct, still in good condition, that supplied the water for the city. On the ride from the station to the hotel we were so pleased with the looks of everything that as soon as we had gotten rooms and washed up, we engaged an automobile and rode all over the city. I was agreeably surprised to find Rome such a clean, pretty place. Unlike Naples, the streets are not so narrow and dirty and only in places is the congestion bad. There are no wide boulevards and avenues lined with trees like Paris or Washington, but then Rome wouldn't be true to Italy if the streets were wide or even straight for any considerable distance. The city is old all right, but its age is not too conspicuous, and the newer public buildings and handsome homes give it a thoroughly modern setting, and unless one knew that it was Rome and without seeing some of the old ruins, they would never imagine that they were in one of the oldest cities in the world. The present is so well blended with the past that I didn't feel as I did at Pompeii that I had stepped backward over the span of years into the center of life of a long past age, but rather that I was looking at it from a distance through the glasses of modern civilization. Rome has outgrown the traditional seven hills of the time of Romulus and Remus, and there are so many hills now that it is difficult to tell which are the original seven. Also, it most certainly was not built in a day nor is it possible to see it all in a measly three days.

Our driver became absolutely disgusted with us because we didn't want to stop at every pile of ruins and listen to a forty-five minute spiel from him about who built it and when, what it was used for, the names of all the old Romans who had made it sacred by crossing its threshold, all its dimensions and how much it weighed and the exact number of people who had been to see it. He thought we lacked appreciation of Roman history when we would tell him to "drive on" to some lively restaurant or take us up some pretty street where there were lots of people. We were duly impressed at the sight of all the famous ruins but we were reserving our official sight-seeing tour for the next day and besides it is a poor policy to listen to a long line of talk about Nero or Caesar or anyone else when the taxi meter is running up a bill. Every time we came to an old building he would slow down as if to stop, but we would just ask him what it was and say "Avante," meaning "Drive on, driver."

We had lunch at the Castle of the Caesars, but I don't know where it gets its name, for Caesar never saw it. It is just another one of those things which have sprung up to answer the demands of tourists.

The American women in Rome have established a bureau of welcome and information for visiting soldiers and have headquarters in one of the hotels. We didn't want any information, as it is lots of fun to find your way around alone, but we thought we would see what they could do in the welcoming line so we called in the afternoon, intending to stay only a few minutes, but the first glimpse of the lady on duty made it necessary to rearrange our plans. She wasn't the prettiest woman I have ever seen, but she was rather young and was so distinctly American that I "fell" for her right away. She put away her knitting and began welcoming us in fine fashion, talking with us in the most informal and friendly way and we felt like we had been friends for years. We implored her to go down town and have tea with us, but she compromised by inviting us to go home and have tea with her, saying that she must be there at her daughter's supper time. We were tickled to death to go home with her, but when she mentioned "daughter" we nearly fainted. We hadn't caught her name and she looked so young that I didn't believe her until we got there and saw her little ten-year-old girl, who was quite as attractive as her mother and she had light hair which is such a rare thing in this country. She served delicious tea and we had another jolly hour of conversation. (Her husband wasn't at home.) She was from Kentucky and had married an Italian colonel, having been over here for quite awhile, which proves that the climate keeps one youthful. When we finally tore ourselves away, she expressed her pleasure at having us, saying that she had almost forgotten how American men made love. We hadn't exactly made love to her, but before we found out she was married we hadn't talked entirely about the weather. Also, considering that both of us had sisters near her daughter's age, she permitted us to kiss the little girl goodbye. She was the first American woman we had seen for nearly five months and it was delightful to talk to her, and the little touch of home life meant more to me than all the historic treasures of Rome.

That night we had dinner at a hotel with Tom's uncle, who is in the American Red Cross and happened to be in Rome at that time. After a regular banquet (on the uncle), we went to a vaudeville show which was designed to keep us from thinking about the war. The uncle wasn't so old and crabby as we had feared (Tom hadn't seen him for years), and we had a fine little party.

Next day we fell an easy prey to a guide and did sight-seeing. We went first to the remains of the Forum, which, if you listened to all the guide had to say, would occupy your attention for a day. There isn't much left of it but a crumbling wall and broken pillars, but every stone has a history attached to it.

From there we went to the Coliseum, which we found exactly as it appears in the history text-books, only it is much more immense than one would imagine. It is a great engineering feat and it is a marvel that it has remained standing for so many hundreds of years. We stood where once were the ring-side seats of the F.F.V.'s[1] and looked down upon the scene of the combats between the gladiators, the chariot races, and the horrible persecutions of the Christians, but in place of these interesting sports there is now only a desolate waste, hallowed by these early martyrs to the cause of religion.

Next we saw the Catacombs—long corridors and vaults four stories underground—where the poor wretches who dared call themselves Christians were buried after furnishing amusement to the Roman populace.

Then we went to the Vatican, which is a huge but shapeless mass of stone. Inside are countless corridors, some fully a hundred yards long, lined on both sides with priceless tapestries, statues of bronze, stone and every kind of marble, paintings and mural decorations by the world's greatest masters, all depicting some Bible story or phase of the life of Christ. When we first went in we stopped every few feet to admire some magnificent specimen, but soon saw that we wouldn't get through in a week at that rate and really it would take a week to see everything there with the proper appreciation of its value. There is such a vast number of things to see that you get tired before very long and lose the full effect of many a masterpiece that it is a privilege to see. The Vatican isn't a bit like one would expect it to be. It's an immense building, having something like 11,000 rooms in it, but the part we saw was just a plain, ordinary art gallery.

Then came St. Peter's Cathedral, grand and imposing from the outside and even more magnificent on the interior. It isn't a bit like our idea of a church, being an immense

[1]First Families of Virginia, a humorous reference.

room of huge proportions in the shape of a cross, with no seats or benches to mar the beauty of its wonderful architecture. There are statues of saints all along the walls and at intervals are recesses where the popes are entombed and in front of each is a large statue of that pope. The walls are covered with beautiful decorations which look like paintings, but are really the finest mosaic work in which the various shades and tints are as perfect as any canvas and only by the closest inspection can it be determined that they are not paintings. In one corner is a stone column of the most artistic design and workmanship, said to have been brought from Solomon's Temple and there is a bronze statue of St. Peter, one foot of which has been partly worn away by the kisses of worshippers. In the center is an altar covered with a canopy of bronze which is supported by four bronze columns after those of Solomon's Temple. The dome, said to be the highest in the world, which was designed and executed by Michelangelo, who also did the painting, is truly an incomparable work of art. Underneath the church are the tombs of the Apostles Luke and Thomas (I think these names are correct) and some of the older popes, these tombs resting on the floor of the old Roman Circus. As I said before, there are no seats in the main room, this being used only for the services of Easter and Christmas, but there is a smaller room adjoining which is used for ordinary services, one of which was being held when we were there, and we stopped awhile to hear the boys' choir. In another room are cases containing all the vast treasures of the church, consisting of robes and headdresses for the popes, embroidered with threads of solid gold; the most beautiful vases and incense burners, etc., of gold and platinum set with the finest of precious stones; gifts of every kind from various principalities and sovereigns, countless in number and the smallest one being worth a fortune. Everything was artistic beyond description and represented the most skilled and intricate workmanship, but it doesn't seem right that these things of such fabulous wealth should remain inclosed in cases in a dark room, where they are seldom seen and never used, when half the people of the country haven't enough to eat.

There are also some bones which they say are part of the remains of St. Peter, and a small piece of wood which they actually claim to be a piece of the Cross of Jesus, but whether it is or not I couldn't bring myself to realize or believe that it really was.

The real beauty of the place is not any of the countless works of art, but the room itself—grand beyond any imagination, containing scores upon scores of statues large and small, yet all in the most magnificent proportion, so large that it is difficult to form any conception of it and with nothing to obstruct the view from end to end and still it doesn't impress you as being empty, rather that its wonderful spaces so admirably designed would be spoiled if there were a single thing there to disturb the effect of harmony. Its grandeur and sense of solemnity cast a spell over one as soon as one enters the door and I almost held my breath all the time I was there. I never felt so infinitesimally small in all my life.

Then we came to the Pantheon, the old temple, now used as a tomb for the kings. Raphael and other old masters are entombed there. This building is typical of the architecture of that time and has been preserved in better condition than any other of the old structures. It is circular in form and, aside from the doorway, its only source of light is through an unprotected hole in the roof. We saw the famous Tiber, but it isn't such a howling success as a river.

The prettiest thing in Rome is the new memorial to King Victor Emmanuel.

"This concludes the performance," and I wasn't half sorry, as I had seen and heard enough of history for one day, and although I wouldn't have missed any of it for worlds, I was glad it was over. I wish I knew more about history so that I could better appreciate the things I saw. This is a very poor description of the many famous sights I saw, but there was so much of it that I just can't record my thoughts in any coherent way. It certainly seemed queer to be there on the very ground where Nero, Pericles, Caesar, Marc Antony and such other important characters of history had lived and moved and had their being. I felt as if I must be dreaming and would wake up at any minute. I would be willing to call it a dream if I could wake up and find myself back at 801 Hanover Street with Taylor shaking me and you calling up that breakfast is ready.

That night we saw *Il Trovatore* played by a splendid company. I did not recognize the names of any of the singers, but they were all good. It's an easy matter to put on an opera over here, as everyone sings.

The following day we called at the Embassy to see Ambassador Thomas Nelson Page, but he was having a conference of some kind and asked us to call the next day. Am certainly sorry that we missed seeing him, but he is expected to visit camp shortly and I will make his acquaintance then.

Most of the day we spent in rambling around through the streets, just "Roaming in Rome" and making some necessary purchases that couldn't be had in Foggia. In the afternoon we called on Dr. Whittinghill. He is a very interesting man and his wife is charming. I believe I told you that her mother was a Miss Braxton, of Fredericksburg, and was married at Hazel Hill. They have two nice children—a girl of twelve and a boy of nine—and I wished that they could have a part of our yard to play in. They were very cordial to us, serving tea and cookies and insisting that we stay to dinner, but our train time made it impossible.

Rome is surely a great place and I want to go back before I leave Italy. One important feature that must not be overlooked is the great improvement over other places in the way of girls. There were lots of pretty girls, well dressed and comely, and to show that we haven't forgotten all about our girls at home, we took a second look at all these so as to be better able to compare them with the standard of the world. These girls aren't in it with the American girls, but they are queens in comparison with those of other Italian cities. There was an abundance of food if one had the money to pay for it, but I can't understand how in the world the poor people live. The only apparent shortage was bread and at every meal we had to show our passes, sign our names, give our home address and present station, age, occupation, color of hair and size of shoe before we could get the allowance of 40 grams (about a slice and a half) and we couldn't get more by hook or crook. The only way to get more bread was to go elsewhere and get another meal. You would have to eat three of four meals in order to get enough bread for one.

There is a horde of guides who are glad to welcome you to the city, but they aren't so insistent as in Naples. You see, the war is a great shock to their business and they try to make up for the loss by grafting from the Americans, but these boys aren't so gullible as the tourists of former days and they can speak just enough Italian to say "Niente," meaning "Nothing stirring." An American looks like a gold mine to everybody in Italy, but we have gotten wise to their tricks now, and as one disappointed waitress said, "All Americans are rich, but some are stingy."

Well, spring has officially come and the fields are dotted with dandelions, daisies, buttercups and jonquils, but they aren't so pretty as those in our yard. There is that something in the air which makes a fellow hold his head up and change the tune he is whistling from "I ain't got nobody much" to "The bells are ringing for me and my gal," although the only bells are those in the cathedral down town which ring every afternoon at twilight, and the only girls are the sad, sad specimens of Foggia. The epidemic of spring fever hasn't begun yet, but there is increasing evidence of it. Today is Palm Sunday and as pretty a one as I ever saw. How I would like to be home and go to church with you and hear the "Palms" sung and be there next Sunday and see the grand parade, but I have to take part in the grand parade to Berlin first and I am getting awfully impatient for it to start.

We have just received the first reports of the German drive, which looks like a powerful blow, but everyone is confident that the English can withstand it. God help us if they can't. Why aren't there a million or more Americans there to lend their strength and enthusiasm to the battle and why can't I be one of that million? The instructors think that we should "rest a little longer, birdie, till the wings shall stronger grow," but resting doesn't teach one how to fly. I am still waiting to finish my 2nd Brevet and my restlessness is mounting by leaps and bounds. When we sailed we were congratulating ourselves on our good fortune and thought that we would be at the front in a couple of months. Now we fear that we may not get there at all. The Italian method of training is something that passeth all understanding.

Since the bombing of Naples we have had several air raid scares, but all proved false alarms. One night they called us out at 2 o'clock, but nothing happened except a lot of verbal explosions at having to get up. Having to get up that night made me stronger in my conviction not to fly a bombing machine if I can possibly get another. Bombing is a very important phase of aviation, but it's the last thing I want to do. We have been making extensive preparations for defense and can show them a hot time if they do appear.

I am enclosing a few pictures (10 in number) which the censor may or may not pass. Am sending some others in a letter to Papa, so that some may get through if all do not. They aren't extra good ones, but you may be able to see that I am thriving on spaghetti, oranges and aerial flights. Will have some better views of Rome by the time I write again. No doubt you will infer that I spend most of my time in having my picture taken, but as nearly every fellow in camp has a camera and a careless disregard of wasting films, the clicking of cameras can be heard all day long. Some two weeks ago a famous Italian pilot, Lieut. Brachpapa, who broke the altitude record in an S.I.A. machine for a passenger-carrying plane, was here to give a demonstration of trick flying. There were no less than five hundred pictures taken of him and his flight was delayed a long time while the boys were taking turns at snapping him. Also, about five hundred films were spoiled in trying to catch him in the act of looping, spinning, diving, etc.

Josiah P. Rowe, Jr.

In Italy

8th Aviation Instruction Center
American Expeditionary Forces
April 14, 1918

Dear Mother and All:

Very little to write about this month. I suppose it is up to me to let you know that I am well, hale and hearty, but I refuse to attribute it to macaroni. Last week a cold and sore throat were camped on me, but as that has gone, just let the Germans come along.

It is mighty good of the home folks to write regularly, and as their letters help so much I have decided that victory and worldwide democracy rest largely with the folks back home after all; therefore, keep on writing. You never know what a letter from home means until you get four or five thousand miles away. No matter what a man may be doing—whether it be searching for submarines in the North Sea, fighting the Germans in France, or flying in Italy—his uppermost thought is home.

The few letters we boys get from girls at home seem to indicate that they are preparing the way for a strategic retreat. They just take it for granted that as soon as we landed in France we became involved in entangling alliances with some French baroness, and when we get to Italy our affections are transferred to an Italian countess. They apparently forget that titled ladies do not hang around on street corners waiting for a stranger to fall in love with them. I am afraid there is no chance for us to regain a "status quo ante," especially at the rate girls are now being married. It looks like a regular epidemic of weddings, and it seems that as soon as a fellow gets a commission he goes and gets a wife with it. I notice that many of the A.E.F. boys are following that plan in France, but they are having trouble with it, as the law requires that they present their birth certificate when applying for the marriage license. You need not bother about sending me mine, as the laws in Italy are not so strict.

I will have to keep my foot on the soft, soft pedal hereafter as the American rules of censorship are being enforced and they are far more stringent than the Italian. The Italian censorship was more of a myth than anything else as they never seemed to open a letter much less delete anything. Although we were allowed a great deal of freedom there was no danger of our disclosing any military information for the simple reason that we don't know any. The next time any of you are in Washington please call on Gen. Squier and tell him that there is a bunch of promising aviators here who would like very much to get in the war and who might be able to do some little good up on the French front. Tell him we will forget how our contracts for 1st lieutenancies were treated as "scraps of paper" if he will only let us "do our bit" in France. But even if I don't get a look at the front I will not consider my experience as a failure as I have learned several things that will be a help to me in the future.

I haven't had a flight for so long that I am beginning to wonder how it feels to go up in an aeroplane and if I don't have a crack-up when I get started it will be the most colossal fluke that ever happened. Send me one of those books about HOW TO BE AN AVIATOR, complete in twenty lessons; Use Your Spare Time to Learn This Latest Art. Perhaps I can learn a little about flying from it. Every once in a while I notice the names of fellows who have gotten their training and commission in the States who were miles behind us in ground school. Please tell me, if you can, how the subways in New York were finished in less than 50 years. Darn the blooming censorship—there is something else I want to tell you; but never mind, mother, don't you cry, I'll be an officer by and by in spite of all the drawbacks. But whatever implications are hurled at the censorship you have to admit that it is economical as we don't have to pay postage any more and the boys certainly will not use so much paper in writing to the "one and only."

Cards from friends in Rome reminded us that it was Easter, so there was no chance of forgetting.

Easter came and went as uneventfully as any other monotonous day. It really wasn't Easter though; it was just March 31st. Of course, it was a "Buona Festa" for the Italians and they blossomed forth in their most brilliant regalia and hied away to their signorinas, leaving us to think of other Easters of happier days and say things that shock the Y.M. director. "Buona Festa" it was that the Italians were celebrating. They have so many that it is hard to keep track of them. They begin with the usual holidays of Xmas, New Year's, Easter, July 4th, etc., then come the birthdays of all the Washingtons, Lees and Lincolns of the country, dating back to the time of Romulus and Remus; then they do honor to every saint that you ever heard of and some that you haven't, then they run in a few just for good measure, and they observe a "Buona Festa" with all the vigor of the I.W.W. on Labor Day. A little thing like a war doesn't make the slightest difference. We don't mind when it comes on a bad day, but it's tough to have a perfectly good day wasted and "Buona Festas" nearly always come on good days.

I wish now that I had postponed my trip to Rome until Easter, but experience in the army has taught me never to put off anything when you have the chance to do it. You can never tell just what's going to happen or when, so just as soon as I finished my 1st Brevet I beat it for the station without losing a minute for fear that something might turn up to keep me from going. Just now I am entitled to seven days' leave, but I don't know when or where I will take it. There are so many places to visit that it is hard to decide. I am crazy to go to Venice, but that is impossible now on account of its being in the war zone—looks like they don't want us to get within a thousand miles of anything connected with the war. Still, there are Florence, Milan, and maybe I can get over to Nice and Monte Carlo; but unless something happens I don't think I will go that far this time. As three days are hardly enough to get a good glimpse of Rome and Naples I will probably go back again.

Do you notice how nicely I am learning to "crab"? Well, I find that the army is a great place for learning things. Even if the war should end tomorrow I would have cause enough to "crab" for the next 18 years. But don't get the idea that I am discouraged or downhearted—not a bit of it. I am well and fit and almost as happy as if I had just finished a dinner of home cooking instead of the old spaghetti, or the commandant had just given me a ten-day pass to Paris. I have just come back from the Y.M. where one of the boys, who is an excellent musician, was playing and among other things he played "She's the Sunshine of Virginia", and for the present I am almost as contented as if I were there.

We were highly honored several days ago when King Victor Emmanuel paid us a short visit. He is a small piece of humanity entirely surrounded by admirals, generals, premiers and ministers, but we managed to get a peep at him, as the enclosed photo will indicate. He was terribly hurt because we didn't call on him while in Rome, but he was readily appeased when I promised to visit him on my next leave.

In Italy

A little bit of Heaven has come into our midst lately in the shape of Misses Richards and Morris, of Philadelphia, who conduct the Y.M. canteen. Besides serving hot chocolate, tea and cookies, and on very hot days, ice cream, they have a kind word and a cheering smile for the boys, which we enjoy as much as the eats, not that there is a dearth of smiles in this country, as we get them wherever we go, but there are different kinds of smiles, you know. It sure is nice to go to the Y.M. on a dull afternoon and have a cup of chocolate or tea served by real American ladies. One certainly does not appreciate the superiority of our women until he sees those of other countries. It's unfortunate that they have to stay in such a place as _____, but we cannot let them go away now. If I keep on at the present rate, the English won't have a thing on me when it comes to drinking tea.

You would never think there was a war going on if you could see this camp between the hours of 11 and 3—it looks like Palm Beach in July and feels much the same. The only signs of life are possibly a few fellows playing ball, and some others playing tennis, and soon it will be too hot for that. The Italians are taking their "siesta" and the Americans are reading, writing, snoozing or cussing. It is aggravating because when the sun doesn't shine it is either raining or the clouds are too low for flying and when it does shine the air is too "bumpy." To partly make up for this loss of time we get up at 5 and have flying from 6 to 11, then "repose," and flying from 3 to 7 or 8. So some night about 10:30 or 11 when you are crawling into bed as sleepy as can be, you might think of us as crawling out of bed with the same feeling, and when you wake up the next morning wondering whether you will have oatmeal or strawberries and cream for breakfast, you might reflect that I am just about sitting down to a dinner of "The Italian

Delight"—spaghetti.

I am having the *Stars and Stripes*, the official A.E.F. paper, sent home so that you can see what is going on among the boys in France. It is a dandy little paper and you can get a better idea of the activities and spirits of the A.E.F. from one issue than from all the magazine articles ever written.

Devotedly,

Josiah P. Rowe, Jr.

In Italy

Aviation Corps in Italy
8th Aviation Instruction Center
American Expeditionary Forces
May 14, 1918

Dear Mother and All:

Well, I have been back in camp over a week and still I can't come back to earth; apparently I am ruined for the simple life, routine, and restriction of military service. I just sit around and stare at nothing in such a way that if the keeper of an asylum would see me I am afraid I would spend the rest of my days in Italy in padded cell No. 24395. Why should a delightful vacation be spoiled by a return to the monotony and drudgery of camp? A fellow gets a short vacation and a glimpse of what he is missing and then goes back to camp, where the lid is on tight and this is what he hears. "Get up, you loafers, it's 4:30," or "Well, what are you kicking about? Spaghetti is good for you," or "9 o'clock; lights out and can that chatter." Still, I guess it's the best way to run a war and keep the fellows right.

I want to tell you about the great trip we were able to take during our vacation recently granted us. You know we are entitled to seven days' leave for every four months' service over here, and when my chance came around I took it mighty quick.

Three good fellows went with me—Schwind,[1] of New York; Thompson,[2] of New Jersey, and Pruitt,[3] of Maryland. After a tiresome night trip we reached Naples about 8 A.M. and spent the morning with barbers, bootblacks and bathtubs. We had nothing definite to do and we had such

[1] 2nd Lt. Everett E. Schwind.
[2] Capt. George M. Thompson, 638th Aero Squadron.
[3] 2nd Lt. David S. Pruitt.

79

a good luncheon that we spent most of the afternoon stuffing, and it surely felt good to be able to sit down in a good hotel and order what we had a craving for. There are many limitations to one's desires—we have stopped asking for milk or butter, and we are glad enough to get sugar—but the choice between two dishes is a source of great joy to us, and good cooking is not to be despised.

The main opera was closed, so at night we were inveigled into attending a musical comedy, which was profoundly rotten. The Italians are fine on opera, but their idea of comedy is pathetic; I'm cured.

Next day we went to Pompeii for a couple of hours, had lunch and then got two cabs and started for Sorrento. We didn't know how far it was, but really didn't care and the three hours' drive, skirting the coast of the Bay of Naples, was all too short. The country is very mountainous, rising almost vertically from the water, and in many places there is scarcely room enough for the road between the towering hills and the edge of the cliff, from which there is a sheer drop of two or three hundred feet to the water. The hills were covered with a profusion of fruits and flowers of every kind and description—a perfect riot of color—and the roadway was lined with handsome villas of various tints of red, brown and yellow, each surrounded and almost covered by a mass of beautiful plants. They say that April showers bring May flowers, but tell me what brings the April flowers! If the March winds had anything to do with it, they certainly made a howling success. I have never seen nature so gorgeously arrayed.

We saw Sorrento long before we got there and decided that there was the Italy of fiction. It is only a small town situated on a little plateau facing the sea and surrounded on three sides by huge mountains making an almost perfect amphitheater. The view from Sorrento is the most magnificent I have ever seen, with mountains above, flowers all around, the sea below, and just across the bay, Naples and Mt. Vesuvius, a cluster of white clouds around its top and a rim of little white villages at its base. The water is the most gorgeous shade of blue—not the blue that the poets write about, but real sure enough blue, and I don't think that it would be amiss to say it is navy blue. This must be the place where they get the bluing.[4]

Our hotel was excellent, being located on the edge of a cliff rising perpendicularly from the water and surrounded by a wonderful garden of orange, lemon, and olive trees, and a countless variety of flowers. At night it was entrancing, even intoxicating, with moonlight on the hills and water, the sound of waves breaking on the shore, Vesuvius dimly outlined like a phantom, with a faint yellow glow above the crater, and the fascinating odor of roses, honeysuckle and wistaria. Italy is said to be romantic, but I never thought so until that night. The man who wouldn't be romantically affected by such a heavenly environment must be hopelessly soured on the world. And no wonder this country has produced such great operas. I felt like writing an opera myself that night as I sat late in the hotel garden, and if the other boys hadn't dragged me off to bed I might have inflicted on you a tender and touching poetic composition. There was only one thing lacking to satisfy my every desire and I don't need to tell you what it was.

The people around Sorrento are of a much higher type than those of this section, the most noticeable difference being that they don't show such an apathy for soap and water. The chief occupation is fishing and the women get to be awfully husky from pulling in the nets. They also do a lot of lace work which may or may not be good. You may judge by the two packages which are now on the way.

[4]A whitening agent similar to bleach.

We were the first American soldiers to go around that way and if curiosity really killed the cat, these people ought to be mighty sick. You would think that a circus had come to town by the crowds that gathered every time we came out on the streets and it really looked like a parade with a whole mob of humanity following us everywhere we went. When I went in for aviation I was not more closely examined than I was in the minute inspection at Sorrento.

In our schedule we had allotted only one day to Sorrento, but it took us two days to make up our minds to leave and then it was with reluctance. We took the boat for Capri and on the way over met a very nice American lady, who has lived in Naples for several years. She insisted that we should go to the boarding house where she was staying and she didn't need to ask us twice, because when anything like home is mentioned we're right on the job. The place was run by an English woman and was well stocked with people, English, American, and Italian, who took us in as members of the "family." We met lots of interesting people, chief among them being a very fine American girl from Maine, who sings in the opera at Naples, a peach of an English girl from the British Embassy in Rome, and a dainty little Italian girl from Florence, who had been doing hospital work all winter and was on her vacation.

Capri is not what you might call a regulation island— it's just a bunch of mountains sticking up out of the water. It is just as attractive as Sorrento. The town, or rather village, is scattered around over the hills, the main part being situated on a little stretch of only medium hilly ground which gives a reasonable assurance that the houses will not roll over and tumble down into the water.

The next morning the three girls and the four of us set out to climb Mt. Salaro, which is about eight or nine hundred metres high and doesn't miss being perpendicular by more than four degrees. I have said before that our uniform with its high, stiff collar was impractical, but I never said it so violently as I did that day. I'll resign before I climb another mountain in regulation uniform. Our progress was necessarily slow and even more so than the terrain demanded as every few yards we wanted to stop and talk to the girls. You can't imagine what fun it is to be with nice, jolly girls and be able to talk with them in something besides the sign language until you have been wholly isolated from them for six months. We finally got to the top and after a short rest started rolling and falling down. All during the descent we whooped and yelled and sang and laughed like a bunch of wild men, and the natives must have thought that the war was over or else the Germans had come, but they found out their mistake—just three attractive girls and four hilarious Americans. We got back "home" with ravenous appetites just in time for a swell dinner. (They call it lunch but its proportions earn for it the right to be called dinner.)

That afternoon we went in a sail boat to the Blue Grotto, which is a most extraordinary phenomenon. You have to lie flat in the bottom of a small boat in order to get through the narrow opening which is the only source of light for the large cave. The water is about sixty feet deep but is of such a clear, delicate shade of blue that the bottom can be seen perfectly. The reflected light on the walls and roof of the cave gives them a ghastly color that makes the place uncanny and when the waves from the outside come washing up over the entrance you wonder how in the world you are ever going to get out. You subconsciously heave a sigh when the boat slides out into the world again. The water all around the island is the same rich blue as at Sorrento and we were crazy for a swim but it was rather chilly and if we had gone in we would have been bluer than the water when we came out.

That night we had a musical picnic—the American girl played and sang, the Italian played and sang, the English girl played and we all sang. About ten o'clock we coupled up and went for a walk in the moonlight. I drew the Italian girl, a Signorina G_____. Her father is a colonel, her brother is a lieutenant, and she has been doing hospital work for two years. She went to school in England for two years and speaks the language quite well, but never until that night had she been alone with a man. You know, in the better families in Italy a couple is never without a chaperone until after the marriage. The Italians must have a lot of fun making love to a girl with an old-maid chaperone sitting on the other end of the sofa. It's a mystery to me how they ever get married over here. I still feel highly flattered that her aunt decided to stay in that night.

Well, you have never seen anything as shy as that girl was at first—she didn't know what in the world to do or say. It being her first experience and to have an American to initiate her was no small test, and while it was an extraordinary event for her it was none the less unique for me. I don't remember ever having been with a girl who had never been out before and I didn't know what in the dickens was expected of a fellow in Italy. I certainly could not feel at ease when I knew that all mankind and Americans in particular were being judged by me. We started off with the usual topics and the war, and the conversation gradually resolved itself into a general discussion of America and Italy. Some of her impressions of the States would make you laugh. She didn't think that there were Indians and cowboys on Broadway, but she did think that New York society life was typical of the entire country. She asked all about the gay life of the "Four Hundred" (of which I knew nothing) and was noticeably disappointed when I had to confess that I had never seen a cabaret show. She couldn't believe that anyone in America ever went to bed before 3 A.M. She asked why there were so many divorces and I said because it is a free country and that was the only way some men could get their freedom. Then she wanted to know why, if it was a free country, there should have been a civil war and why so many states had prohibition. I told her that it was free in a certain sense, but there had to be some restrictions on personal liberty. She replied that there didn't seem to be any on La Follette and the German agents. I told her that she was laboring under a misapprehension and she asked who she was. You can't argue with a person like that. She had never heard of Ty Cobb, Christy Matthewson or Jim Jeffries, but she was a great admirer of Mary Pickford and said that she thought Buffalo Bill was one of our finest characters. She didn't know whether Bryan was an opera singer or the name of a state. I told her it was a state—a more or less unsettled state of mind. She asked what was the ideal place of the country and I told her it was Fredericksburg. Can you believe that she never heard of it? Have the Chamber of Commerce send her one of those illustrated booklets. She said that she had always wanted to go to Nebraska to see the great fields of wheat, but I told her they were no different from the fields of gently swaying spaghetti.

She wanted to know all about Niagara Falls, Yellowstone Park, the Grand Canyon, the cotton fields of Georgia, the ranches of Idaho, New Orleans molasses, Smithfield hams and Stafford watermelons, and what I didn't know I had to make up for her. Why didn't I join the "See America First" movement? We talked about government of the people, by the people, and for the people, labor unions, protective tariff, government ownership of railroads, states' rights, crooked politics in West Virginia, taxation without representation, Roosevelt, etc., almost everything except what a fellow usually talks about to a girl. Every time I would use a slang expression she would check me up on it and I would flounder and try to explain it to her. I don't know how well she enjoyed the evening, but she found out that men were perfectly harmless and she began to wonder why girls over here are so closely guarded. She is a mighty nice little girl but don't be looking for me to bring her home as a souvenir.

Capri is an ideal place for a lazy man to live. About the only work there is to do is to keep the fruits and flowers from growing right on in the front door and the women do all that. The men have a soft life; just sit around in the sunshine smoking long clay pipes and wait until meal time. They appear to think that unless they sit tight the island will float away. Once or twice I did see a man in motion; the first time to shoo a fly off his nose, and the second to light his pipe. There must be a law against a man doing any kind of work as when we arrived there was a score of women who refused to let us land until we had handed over our suitcases. They tossed them up on their heads and carried them all the way up to the house—for two cents. It is a common sight to see them with a box, basket, or barrel of stuff beautifully balanced on their beans, climbing up the mountain side as though it were as level as a tennis court. With such a delicate sense of balance they should make fine aviators.

The girls are by far the prettiest I have seen in Italy. Just plain, unadorned beauty but nearly everyone called for a second look so that about half the time I was walking backwards. Besides the usual shining black hair and sparkling eyes, most of them have the most marvelous complexions which might be taken for camouflage except that the drug stores don't look very prosperous. A "You just know she wears them" store would go bankrupt in two weeks on that island and a shoe dealer would be about as useless as a fruit merchant. Such articles as Bon-Ton, American Lady and Lily of France are not much in vogue this season, either. They are a happy, contented crowd and go about their duties with a smiling face and a merry song. Would it be permissible to say that they are CAPRI-cious? These people never lose any sleep over compulsory education and they don't care a hang about the self-determination of peoples—they have already determined that they are absolutely satisfied.

We left Capri at 7 A.M. and, fortunately enough, the English girl was returning to Rome the same day. With her along an otherwise tiresome trip was made highly enjoyable and we forgot to grumble about the square wheels on the train. We spent several hours in Naples, had luncheon there, and reached Rome about 11 P.M., just in time to find the first three hotels we went to crowded. We had intended to do a lot of sight-seeing but had previously seen so many old ruins that we couldn't work up any enthusiasm, especially as it was raining, and so the idea was abandoned.

The English girl, a Miss _____ (don't judge her by her name), rustled up three others and we took several luncheons and dinners with them. They were a "jolly ripping" bunch and after meeting them I don't wonder that England is such a great nation. Miss _____ was doing government work in Petrograd all during the revolution and another had been nursing in Malta for two years; another had served in India and Egypt, and the fourth was on a special mission from "dear old Lunnon." They were fine girls and when we congratulated them upon their work, they said in the most matter of fact way, "Well, we just had to do

something." All have brothers or sweethearts in the service
and if you could see the girls you wouldn't marvel that the
English fight so splendidly. One of Miss _____'s brothers
was taken prisoner by the Turks when Kut-el-Amara was
captured.

After dinner one night we went to see *Intolerance* and
it was certainly well named. We couldn't tolerate more
than two reels of it and then went to see the Forum and
Coliseum by moonlight. It was surely an impressive sight,
but it is no place for a nervous or superstitious man. The
next night we went to a second-rate opera called *La Fa-
vorita*. It may have been somebody's favorite but certainly
not mine. It was just our luck for the main opera to be
closed. They played *Mignon* the night before we arrived
and *Tosca* the night after, but during the three days we
were there it was closed for repairs.

We called on Mrs. _____ and had a delightful luncheon at her home. Any kind of American woman is a welcome sight to us, but she would take a blue ribbon in any
beauty show. I knew that sugar was awfully scarce in Rome
so before leaving F_____ I had gotten several pounds for
her, by means of a little graft, and she was as glad to see
it as I would be to see some of you.

We called twice to see Ambassador Page, but the first
time he was out and the second time he was engaged in a
conference with Signor Marconi. I told the secretary that
I wouldn't mind seeing him, too, but there was nothing
doing.

Thompson and I went around to see the Whittinghills
and found that Dr. Whittinghill was off on a tour of small
towns and his wife was going through agony at the den-
tist's. We stayed about an hour talking to the children and
enjoyed it immensely. You never saw anyone so proud to
be Americans as those children are. George is the most

enthusiastic little chap I ever met and he just raves over the way we are going to win the war. He displayed with pride a large American flag of his own and when I asked him if he was going to hang it out of the window on July 4th, he asked what that was. How is that for a real, live American boy who thinks more of his nationality than most kids? It's a shame that those children can't stay in America and go to school instead of attending the Italian schools. Diana is a sweet little girl and as bright as any child I ever knew. She entertained us like a regular lady. I took them a box of candy and the enclosed letter shows how much they appreciated it.

Here we are back at camp at "The End of Seven Perfect Days" in Naples, Sorrento, Capri, and Rome, but the air is fine this week and flying is good. I got up to 8,000 feet, my highest yet—and had lots of fun doing spirals and gliding down in that vast space where there is no sound except the wheezing of the air as it rushes by.

We have Italian movies once in a while and these help us miss America more than ever. They showed a comedy last night that all but moved us to tears; I haven't the heart to attempt one of their tragedies. No doubt the Italians would go crazy if they could see Charlie Chaplin, provided his line of fun didn't go over their heads. We were fortunate enough to get a Mary Pickford picture some time ago, and although it was about four years old it was good to see a familiar face.

Josiah P. Rowe, Jr.

8th Aviation Instruction Center
American Expeditionary Forces
June 2, 1918

My dearest Mother:

Well, you see I have it and I am the happiest fellow in camp today. I got my R.M.A.[1] yesterday and my commission today, from which you will infer that red tape has been eliminated from G.H.Q., but not so. The War Department decided about six weeks ago that we had been the unfortunate victims of adverse circumstances and that if any group of men in the whole United States Army deserved commissions it was us. So they sent along the commissions regardless of our flying status and they just arrived today. I had not won my R.M.A. at the time the recommendations were sent in so my commission reads NON-FLYING. That's fine for an aviator who has been flying six months. However, I will be put on flying status in a week or two.

My official designation now is Josiah P. Rowe, Jr., 2nd Lieut. A.S. SIG. R.C.R.M.A., U.S.A., 8th A.I.C., A.E.F., P.D.Q., R.S.V.P., S.O.S., C.O.D. No communications will be considered unless addressed according to the above. While I am an officer, duly accredited and vouched for, theoretically I will remain a cadet until I am ordered to active service. This is just a military form and should be coming through in about two weeks.

I am not an angel by any means, and hope that I won't be one for a long, long time, but nevertheless I now wear wings, wings of silver, shoulder bars of gold, a watch of nickel, identification tag of bronze and buttons of brass. If

[1]Reserve Military Aviator.

you could see me now you might think I was the display counter of a jewelry store.

I have been waiting for my commission for so long (over a year) and there have been so many delays and disappointments that its importance had been greatly magnified and so the ceremony of receiving it was a sad failure and decidedly flat. I don't feel a bit bigger than before and I certainly cannot fly any better. The greatest difference is that as a cadet I didn't have to be so scrupulously careful about matters of dress. In the good old days a spot or two on my uniform never caused me any loss of sleep, but now even a speck of dirt is apt to bring a court-martial. I think I will start wearing aprons to insure a clean, immaculate appearance. A little mud on my shoes was formerly a matter of no consequence, but now if they don't glisten like a mirror there's no chance of the Allies winning the war. As a private, the government was good enough to provide uniforms, equipment, and three meals a day, but now I have to furnish these necessities myself. I'm not so sure that I want to be an officer after all, but I guess I won't resign, as a man seems to be often judged by the decorations on his shoulders.

Of far more concern to me is that I have finished the course of preliminary training. I have been flying continually for the past two weeks and some of the flights were quite interesting. Most of them were climbing exercises, going to a certain height, two or three thousand metres, and spiralling down. One exercise was to climb for forty-five minutes, on which I had a dandy good machine and got up to 4,000 metres. This is not a world's record by any means, but it is pretty good for the type of planes used here. The most difficult exercise was "shooting for the square," that is the rectangle, about 50 by 100 yards. The student goes up to 1,200 metres, cuts, glides down and tries to land, letting the wheels touch inside the square and not letting the machine run outside. This is not an easy stunt, especially as the square is just beyond some hangars which seem to rise up in your path like a bugaboo and make you think that you can't possibly get over them without using the motor, which makes the shot void. Most everyone overshoots about 200 yards at first, but after six trial shots it isn't so hard unless there is a strong wind.

The last flight was the best of all, being a cross-country flight in two laps, 97 and 66 miles respectively. It was fearfully hot when I started up, but still I was bundled up like an Eskimo and when I got up high I fervently wished that I had put on a few more sheepskin garments or else had brought along a stove. My hands became numb and I was cold all over—all except my feet. You can't imagine what great difference there is in temperature between a spot on the ground and a point two or three thousand metres directly above it. On a very hot day when you have been perspiring profusely and are worn out with swatting flies, it is certainly refreshing to go up high enough to see the snow away across the mountains, and to look far out into the Adriatic and think about how nice it would be to go down and take a swim. But this time I went a good deal higher than usual and stayed there for quite a long time.

I started out and climbed up to 4,100 metres (about 13,500 feet), the highest I have yet been, and when I looked down I thought surely something was wrong with my eyesight. I had a map, and locating the town of A, thirty miles distant, I headed for it; but it seemed as if I would never get there, in fact it was hard to tell that I was moving at all. Except for the wind driving against my face I couldn't detect any signs of motion. Really, it gets monotonous when up so high and flying in a straight line. I sat there and sang to myself to keep my ears from clogging up until the earth slowly moved along under me. I went from camp to "A," out over the sea to "B" and back to camp.

When about five miles from camp I had the delightful sensation of hearing my motor sputter and gasp and finally poop out entirely. But, as always, altitude is your best friend and I was able to glide into camp without mishap. If I hadn't been so high I might have landed in somebody's barnyard or front door. (They are hard to distinguish.)

Then I got another bus and went off on the second lap. I started this flight as an "Aspirante" and came back a "Pilote Superiore," which shows that I did learn something, although I thought I knew all about aviation beforehand. There were a lot of white, snowy clouds and I had quite an interesting time dodging the big ones and going through the smaller ones. It's dangerous to stay in a cloud very long, as you lose all sense of direction and balance and while you think you are flying perfectly level you are apt to come out standing on your ear. The poets are all wrong—there's nothing silvery about the inside of a cloud. It's just like a very dense fog and is full of "bumps."

I am glad to get it all over with for many reasons, but the principal one is that I have a pretty good chance of being sent to France—not to the front. Alas, there must be more training. Judging from the time I have spent in training I ought to be some good when I eventually get through. But still this will be a step in the right direction. There is more action there in a week than here in a year; besides I will have a chance to fly a type of machine that appeals to me far more than the ones used here. I may be sent in a week, maybe a month and maybe longer, but I am pulling for the best. I will cable you when I leave.

We have had a change of commandants lately and the new one is quite human. He has decided (as I did months ago) the restrictions of camp and the unattractiveness of this town are not conducive to a high morale among soldiers, especially aviators, and has inaugurated a system of weekend passes to Naples whereby a certain portion of the men not actively engaged in flying can leave here Friday afternoon, go to the opera, get some good food, see some nice people, go swimming, and have a jolly time generally, returning to camp on Monday morning in better spirits and better fitted for flying because of the diversion. Naples itself isn't the most attractive city in the world, but its environments are wonderful and if I don't go to France too soon I expect to have some pleasant times over there. Of course this announcement caused great elation among the fellows, but this was mild compared to a demonstration that was held a few days ago. Rumors were whispered around that a bunch of American cooks were en route to this camp to rescue us from the agonies and perils of Italian cooking. We were a little dubious at first—it was too good to be true—but the rumor persisted and as the day for their arrival approached we began to make elaborate preparations for their reception. On the eventful day the entire command marched to the station and drew up in parade formation. Sure enough they did come—15 of them—and they were taken bodily from the train and placed in a gaily bedecked carriage drawn by four fiery steeds. Then, headed by a band, we marched all over town, yelling and cheering like maniacs. Reaching the camp, they left the carriage and were shown all the wondrous beauties of the camp, preceded by a detail of men who scattered pretty flowers along the path. Then the C.O. made a speech of welcome, after which we danced and sang and hugged and kissed them until they thought we were plain nuts. That night we stormed the kitchen, captured the Italian cooks, made them ride the rail all around camp, and then put them in the jug for the night. We tried to punish them by forcing them to eat some of their own delicious spaghetti, but they liked it too well. Next morning at sunrise they were lined up against the wall and executed with "neatness and dispatch." Now we have a regular mess, good food, well cooked, and everybody has a smile that won't come off.

I have just received your letter written on Mother's Day, which made me feel both good and bad. I appreciate your kind thoughts, but it hurts me to think that the occasion came and went without my writing to you. Unfortunately we knew nothing about it until two weeks after it had passed. But every day is Mother's Day with me now. Maybe it didn't used to be, but not a day goes by now that I don't think of you and when I get back I will do something besides think. So long; love to all.

Devotedly,

Josiah

"Here's where we got our start." (The School of Military Aeronautics at Princeton University.)

"A memory."

The RMS *Adriatic*.

"Destroyers on the job."

October 31st, 1917.

R.M.S."ADRIATIC".

MENU.

Consommè Dubelloy   Potage Bagration

Turbot, Shrimp Sauce

Compôte of Pigeon, Americaine

Prime Ribs and Sirloin of Beef, Horseradish

Vegetables   Boiled Potatoes

Braised Loin of Veal, Bristol

Salad : Persil

Fig Pudding   Almond Cakes

Dessert   Coffee

A grounded observation balloon in Paris.

Porthole view of Liverpool.

Australian troops.

"French kids."

An army truck.

The troop transport train from France to Italy.

The Eiffel Tower.

"On the way to Italy."

Campo Sud, Foggia.

Josiah
in Foggia.

"Vive Italia, Vive America"

"My bunk."

"Doing my first Giro."

A Caudron trainer.

A Maurice Farman trainer.

Josiah's flight instructor, Pezzoli.

"A squadron of Nieuports."

Dutch Krueger in Foggia.

Josiah in Foggia.

1st Lt. Leroy Kiley who flew Caproni bombers in combat.

"Caproni warming up." The Caproni bomber had three motors, 450 horse-power, and went 90 mph.

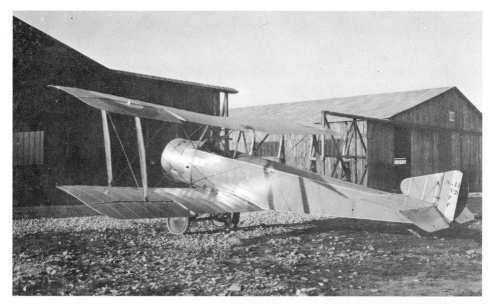

Sopwith 1¹/₂ Strutter.

Flight instructor Pettrucci (left), with "Freddie", presumably a student.

2nd Lt. Tom Ewing.

"Trowbridge."

An S.I.A. 7B

King Victor Emmanuel of Italy (center) on his visit to the camp in Foggia.

Starting a Nieuport by hand.

"Tenente Brachpapa [center], Italy's most daring pilot."

"Ted Krom in Pomilio."

"Ready for Austrian raiders."

A Sopwith tri-plane.

Josiah in his flight gear.

A cheerful group.

"Capitano Albertoni."

"How do they fly?"

"Dry land sailing."

"War or no war, baseball must go on."

"Our own design."

A motorcycle with sidecar.

"This is the Fly Swatter Brigade which achieved many notable victories in that ne'er to be forgotten Battle of Foggia."

"Inspection."

"Raise you five."

"Rolling the bones."

"Rolling snowballs."

"Picking rocks." (To clear the airfield).

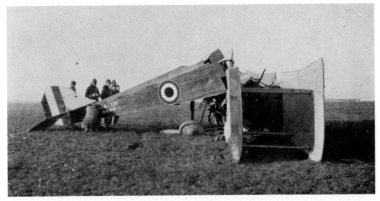

"A plain error and an aero-plane."

"A new way of putting a machine in a hangar."

"Smith makes a neat job."

"This motor will never mote again."

"A group of motoristes."
(Mechanics.)

A rotary plane engine.

"Bringing in the sheaves."

"My chambermaid and the best Italian I ever knew. You should have seen the old fellow cry when I left."

Italian soldiers and sailors.

"Motoring in Foggia."

"Carry packages and win the war.
Good head work."

A public well in Foggia.

A street scene in Foggia.

"Lawnmowers
at work."

"A load of fuel."

"Going to town on Saturday."

A family in Foggia.

"Tom Ewing and me in Roma.
Puzzle—why the smiles?"

"Schwindy and me and the *old* Roman chariot
we traveled in from Pompeii to Sorrento."

The Isle of Capri from atop Mt. Salaro.

"Mt. Salaro. Reposo and vino
rosso."

A scene in Rome.

"The noblest Roman of them all."

In France

U.S. Air Service, France
June 28, 1918

My dearest Mother:

Well, I have been back in La Belle France over a week
and I think I have sufficiently recovered from the tortures
of our six day trip to tell you a little about it. First of all,
let me say that all the horrors of war are not in the trenches.
Few things are worse than a long trip in these European
trains when you are wedged in a narrow little compartment
with anywhere from four to seven (usually the maximum)
fellow sufferers. Still, we managed to live through it by
having a jolly crowd, frequent stops, and a willingness to
suffer any hardships that would get us out of Italy. When
we crossed the border I didn't see anyone shedding tears.

We all hoped we would go up by way of Rome, Florence, and Genoa with long stopovers in each place, but
instead we went by the same route that we came down
last fall (west coast) and reached Bologna just in time to
miss a train that would enable us to stop in Milan for a
day and night. From Torino up to the border and for a long
time in France we passed through that beautiful mountainous country and it made me sore because I couldn't look
out of both sides of the train at the same time.

Almost the first thing we saw in France were Sammies[1]
(they hate the name but I don't know what else to call
them) and we have been seeing them ever since. We went
up and spoke to these first ones like they were friends from

[1]A term for American soldiers in France.

home and in fact they were because we hadn't seen any for so long. When we went through France last fall we saw a few but this time there were thousands and thousands. There are few stations where they are not in evidence and the roads and fields don't look natural now unless you see groups of our soldiers. As we went deeper into the heart of the country we began to see ever increasing signs of America's participation. More and more soldiers, American locomotives, American supplies on the trains, American cigarette boxes along the tracks, and American slang around the stations. At one station there was an American canteen operated by good-looking American girls where they served WHITE bread and coffee. Honestly, it tasted like cake to us. Nothing but our bashfulness prevented us from falling on their necks both for the bread and for their own sweet selves.

We stopped in one town where they have headquarters of a certain branch of the service and there are so many Americans that truly it looks like an American town with the French as visitors. You go into a hotel and are met by an American clerk. You pick up an American telephone and a cheerful businesslike voice says, "number please." Between two cities there is a daily train known as the "American Special," entirely equipped and operated by Americans, and it makes these French trains look like toys. The people will never get used to its deep-toned whistle so unlike the peanut-roaster kind. All these things and the many other indications that we are most certainly in the war were positively bewildering to us who for such a long time were so out of touch with our progress that sometimes while in Italy we almost forgot that there was a war going on.

Now we are in a dandy little Casual Camp in a lovely section of the country. _____ is the name of the town, which the army designates under the very descriptive title of A.S.R.C.B., S.O.S., A.P.O. 725.[2] We have nice quarters, good shower baths, and corking good meals. Just think of ham and eggs, buckwheat cakes, maple syrup, and genuine coffee with milk and sugar for breakfast. Then for dinner beefsteak, mashed potatoes, green peas, apple dumpling, white bread, butter, lemonade, and lettuce from the camp garden. Really, it all seems too good to be true. The mess of the men is just as good but now and then we hear the mess sergeant gets a balling out. These birds don't know a good thing when they see it. Just as a reminder of olden days, they served macaroni one day but it was so nicely prepared that we didn't recognize it.

The only kick I have about the camp is that it is a Casual, or Rest, Camp. The other was little more, so I am fed up on Rest Camps. We expect daily to be sent to a school for advanced flying and they can't make me mad by doing it "toute de suite." I have learned many things in the army but I don't think I will ever learn to wait and do it gracefully. Still, it is joy supreme to hear the first notes of reveille, give a grunt and turn over for another snooze. Oh, boy, it's a great life. It's fun all right but it makes me feel like a cheat. An aviator is supposed to fly and I am game whenever they give me a chance.

The town is a marvel of neatness and cleanliness compared to those of Italy and the people are very interesting. You can't imagine how really charming the French are until you have been with Italians for seven months. We have movies at the "Y" nearly every night and the people, old and young, come in droves. They are more than cordial to us and in the afternoons there are few doorsteps and front yards not occupied by smiling Sammies going through vocal acrobatics in their daily parlez vous lesson with some

[2]St. Maxient, France.

bright little Suzanne, Yvonne or Annette. The country is very attractive, not so extensively cultivated as Italy, but abounding in beautiful green trees and bushes, which are so rare in most parts of Italy.

I haven't heard from Reg yet, although I expect a letter in every mail. I had forgotten the number of his hospital and in one town in which we stopped I looked all through there in hopes of finding him, but in vain. At one hospital the Doc said, "Sure, he's here. Right up on the second floor." I was up the steps in one bound, only to find it was some bird from Montana. I gave him a pack of smokes because of his name and because he appeared so sorry to have been the cause of my unconcealed disappointment. I am quite sure that Reg will be sent here upon recovery for reassignment to a squadron and I am hoping that he will come before I leave.

Many of the fellows have met friends of old and Tom Ewing (I have mentioned him before) had the good fortune to meet two girl friends on the way up, but no such luck for me. I have seen lots of old Ft. Meyer fellows but I haven't experienced that wonderful sensation of meeting a friend from home.

I have been reading with special interest of the Italian successes and the participation of a detachment of American flyers from our camp, and that one of them, Young,[3] from Des Moines, has been captured. He was a fine chap and I hate to think of the hard times he will probably have at the hands of the Austrians.

Probably you will not understand why I am so anxious to be transferred to France just about the time some of our men are getting into action. Well, there are lots of things you won't understand until I get back home, but I will say that we took the course that would enable us to get to the

[3]1st Lt. Clarence M. Young.

front with the least possible delay. I would go to Borneo if it would hasten the time when I could take an active part in the fight.

Best love and regards to everybody.

Devotedly,

Josiah P. Rowe, Jr.

2nd Aviation Instruction Center
on Active Service with the
American Expeditionary Forces
July 15, 1918

My dearest Mother:

I guess you think that I have forgotten all about you during the last couple of weeks, but far from it. The main trouble is that the habits and customs of Italy have left their imprint upon me, and I can't so quickly accustom myself to the American way of doing things in a hurry. Just think of living six months under a system which left you more time than you knew what to do with, and then be suddenly required to conform to a schedule which allows only two hours spare time each day, which must necessarily be devoted to sleep, and you will cease to wonder why I haven't written. A day like this doesn't permit of much billet-douxing. Reveille 3:45. Breakfast 4:00. Flying 4:30 to 10:30. Drill and calisthenics 10:30 to 12:00. Dinner 12:00. Sleep 12:30 to 3:00. Flying 3:00 to 9:30. Lights out 10:00—good night.

It's pretty strenuous, all right, but it sure is a "Win the War" schedule. If we could have persuaded the Italians to adopt such a system I might be now telling you about thrilling trips over the lines, but as it is you will have to continue to get your information from the magazines for two or three months.

Another reason why there have been no letters is that everything is more or less unsettled and if I should have written you a letter one night based on the information and "dope" in force at the time I would have awakened in the morning to find it all wrong. Lightning changes are very much in vogue and half the time I don't know whether I'm going or coming.

I arrived here on July 1st, started flying the next day and completed the course on the 11th. It wasn't hard at all—just enough training to get us accustomed to another type plane. The next day I had orders to go to St. Max to await assignment to another school, being allowed three days extra time to make the trip. Visions of Paris flashed across my mind and I found myself extremely fortunate in being able to witness the grand fete on the 14th. It was an opportunity of a lifetime and I feared it must be too good to be true. While checking my baggage for gay Paree, and with but fifteen minutes before train time, the now familiar words "Your orders have been changed" were whispered in my ears.

Back at camp, I was told that I should wait here until the 16th and then go direct to the next flying school, but still being permitted to have the three days' extra time. Visions of Paris were washed away by a flood of tears, but I was able to control my grief by the hope of locating Reg in the intervening time. This morning I had a wire from the director of the hospital, giving me his present station. Then I consulted all the maps and railway officials in town and found to my delight that I could get up to his camp, spend a day and night with him and get back to _____ on schedule time. Visions of old Reg and a happy reunion obscured all else and I was in the throes of ecstasy. While affixing my John Henry to a telegram advising Reg of my intended visit the cheering words "Your orders have been changed" were sweetly sung to me by an orderly. The latest is that the three-day feature has been withdrawn and I am to proceed to _____ "by the quickest possible route," but I don't dare state it as a fact, as there are yet about eighteen hours before I leave and my orders may be revoked any number of times.

With the golden opportunity ruthlessly snatched away from me, there is little hope of seeing Reg until I take my next seven days' leave, which lurks somewhere in the dim and distant future. The fact that we are to be shunted around St. Max and the withdrawal of the three-day privilege, while rather discouraging to my plans, indicate that training facilities have been improved and we will lose no time in getting to work on our final training, which has already suffered countless delays. Here's hoping that the "dope" is right and that the days of languishing in camps are ended.

As I said before, I have been kept pretty busy while here, but have managed to get into town on one or two occasions—one on July 4th, when the French joined with us heart and soul in celebrating that great event. Every building in the city was profusely decorated with the Stars and Stripes and the Tricolor and every Frenchman shouted "Vive l'Amerique" until he or she was hoarse. Likewise, on the 14th, when we reciprocated and assisted in honoring their great day.

As I mentioned in my last letter, the city is filled to overflowing with Americans. The streets are packed with them and every available house is utilized for their quarters. At the officers' club they have American servants, American meals with American music and really it is difficult to convince yourself that you are not in some pretty little city in the States. There have been a number of dances at which there were American girls galore, and while I would walk ten miles to see one, I couldn't persuade myself to dance around (as much as I would like to) until 1 or 2 A.M. when I had to fly at 4:30.

In France

I have met quite a few fellows whom I knew in the olden days—Frank Oliver, of Irvington; Doug Lancaster, of Ashland; Sammy Pritchard, of Norfolk, who roomed next to me at V.P.I.; and lots of training camp friends; but it seems like I will have to wait until I get back home to see a good old Fredericksburg face. You can't imagine what it means to always be in search of someone from home, to anxiously scan the countenances of everyone in khaki for some familiar face and to be always disappointed. Evangeline had nothing on me!!!

Devotedly,

Josiah

3rd Aviation Instruction Center
American Expeditionary Forces
August 4, 1918

A perfectly beautiful Sunday is just drawing to a close, but I cannot let it pass without writing to you. I have just finished supper and I am sitting by my bunk in the cool of the evening and an O.D. shirt while the sun gradually lowers behind the line of poplars which forms the western boundary of our camp. We don't fly on Sundays, so I relapsed into habits of old and slept until ten o'clock. Now don't scold, as some extra sleep is essential on a 4 to 10 schedule, and besides, what's the use of being an officer if you don't take it easy on Sundays? Then I went to the "Y" service, at which I had communion for the first time since I left home. After dinner I walked out into the country along the road to Chateauroux with some of the fellows and I got back just in time for supper. The country is gently rolling with frequent patches of woods very much like it is around Blacksburg,[1] and all the roads are lined with tall, slim poplars, the inevitable background of every French landscape. There are countless wheat fields in which the harvest is plenty, but the laborers are few. Many German prisoners are impressed for gathering in the harvest, but there aren't enough. The villages are very quaint and attractive and the French passion for gables and dormer windows is indeed pleasing. When you see an old chateau back from the road and surrounded by a clump of trees you don't know whether you are in front of it or in back

[1]Blacksburg, Virginia, home of his alma mater, Virginia Polytechnic Institute.

or off to one side. All you can see is a confused mass of gables, turrets and sharp angles pointing in every direction, which is a delightful contrast to the painfully heavy types of Italy.

Of course, you want to know something about camp besides that it is A.P.O. 724. In addition to that distinction, it is the largest aviation camp in France, and it is American to the core. The only Frenchman in the camp is the barber and he speaks English. How do you expect us to learn French that way? The camp is what might be called self-supporting and there is little need to go to town (8 miles distant) unless one had a "petite femme" there—which I haven't. I haven't been in since I arrived, although we have our own railway connecting us with "France." Really, this is such an American center that one doesn't have to even close his eyes to imagine himself in the States, although if I were I wouldn't be in a camp.

We have two immense "Y" huts with everything a fellow could desire—large reading and writing rooms, excellent library, games of all kinds, and canteens at which one can get anything from shoe polish to Huyler's chocolates. Cigarettes and tobacco are cheaper than at home. The "Y" is simply plastered with signs such as "Write to your mother-in-law, it pays," etc., etc., and then it goes and has some good entertainment every night, either movies, vaudeville, or band concert. Consequently, I will have to keep away from the "Y" if I am to do anything in the line of correspondence.

I am not sure whether the army or the Red Cross runs this camp. Our relations with the latter are fully as many and as important as with the former. When we fly very early, just stop in the Red Cross dining room and have a cup of coffee and a sandwich. Then, when we come back from the field, run and get some chocolate and jam. For dinner we go to the Red Cross and they surely can serve a good one. In the afternoon if we feel a little empty or thirsty, just step in the Red Cross cafeteria and have cold tea, lemonade or milk with sandwiches and sometimes cakes. At night, after a Red Cross supper, we have a corking nice little club room, in which to read, write, play cards or just sit back in the nice cushioned chairs and gaze out of real curtained windows. If we have a button off our shirt or a slit in our breeches, go to the Red Cross tailor shop and have it fixed in a jiffy by deft and flying fingers (lady fingers). If we want a haircut, shave, shampoo and shine, go to the Red Cross barber shop. (No, we don't have lady barbers.) If you want a shower bath, hot or cold, go to the Red Cross bath house. If we get to thinking about our girl and wonder how she looks when she smiles we just go over and get one of the Red Cross girls to show us. If we wonder if we have forgotten how to dance we go over to the Red Cross some night when there is music and find out that we have. If we want to see a good movie, go to the Red Cross any night. Then, of course, there is the hospital, which takes care of us in case of pinkeye, the heaves, or distemper. Really, the Red Cross is the light and life of the camp and the girls do everything for us except tuck us in bed at night. The prayerful thanks of more than a million men go out every night to the people back home for giving us the Red Cross and Y.M.C.A.

Oh! Yes, there are some military duties to be performed lest you think that this is purely a recreation center. For instance, we fly from 5 A.M. to 10 A.M. and the Nieuport training is pretty strenuous. We have acrobatics, cross-country and formation flying, combat work and aerial gunnery. The acrobatics are all kinds of sports and in the combat work you get all the thrills of actual battle. Two planes equipped with camera guns go up and at a signal the fight is on. Each pilot tries to maneuver his plane into a favorable position, sights on the enemy, and pulls the trigger, and the gun is loaded, too, but with camera plates instead of shells. When each pilot has "downed" the other a sufficient number of times, they come in, have the photos developed, and see who was the victor.

In the afternoon we go to class and learn how to strip and assemble three or four different kinds of machine guns with our eyes shut and our hands tied behind our backs before the instructor can say "Jack Robinson." Also, we have classes in deflection in which we learn how far to "lead" an enemy plane which is 200 yards distant, traveling at 110 miles per hour and the velocity of the bullet being 2,700 feet per second. Then we go to the range for revolver practice, shooting at stationary and moving targets, and to the traps for shooting at clay pigeons, and to the machine gun range for shooting at model aeroplanes flying in all kinds of crazy directions. Then, after studying for examinations, we have nothing to do until tomorrow at 4 A.M. The work is intensely interesting and everyone is on his toes. How I wish that we could have been doing this all the time down in Italy when we had nothing to do but sit around in the sun and figure how many yards of spaghetti we had eaten.

We are flying the prettiest and daintiest little aeroplanes ever built. They aren't much bigger than a bee, but they sure can travel and do every kind of stunt imaginable. There are some of the Liberty planes here also, and believe me they are world-beaters. They look like a million dollars and go faster than a month's salary. You feel like you are on a battleship when you get in one. I may be assigned to the Liberties, and if so you won't hear a whimper out of me and I can show my heels to any German bus, although I don't intend to.

The news from the front these days is certainly encouraging. The Allies are pushing the Germans back in giant strides and the Americans are showing them all that they can do some things besides play baseball, make money and brag. How I would like to be up there in the scrap! When such things are going on it seems awfully insignificant and futile to be in just "training." Haven't you heard that word a lot? I'm sick of it. It looks like the boys who were drafted are the only ones lucky enough to get to the front, while a poor aviator who volunteered over a year ago and has been just boiling over for action is still miles behind the lines, safe in the security of the S.O.S. But I won't have to wait much longer—a month here—perhaps a couple of weeks at another school for aerial gunnery and then—well, if they can think of anything else to detain us with I am going to desert and join the doughboys. There won't be any front for me to go to unless I hurry up. Of course, the present successes have revived arguments as to how long the war will last. Some say that the last seven years of war will be the worst, but others are more cheerful with "Hell, Heaven or Hoboken by Christmas."

Do you sometimes think that I am a poor soldier because I "crab" too much? Well, when down in Italy I did kick a lot, partly because there wasn't much else to do and partly because if I hadn't complained I would have lost my self-respect. Gee! But it was awful to languish in camp down there for endless days and weeks with little to look forward to but more of the same, when other fellows were getting promotions, medals and Germans. It was stifling to ambition and you know how discontent breeds when a bunch of fellows don't have enough to do. All that is gone now, but not forgotten, and prospects are bright and cheerful. I have gotten back with the Americans and caught their all-pervading enthusiasm and I don't think you will hear any more complaints. Just because I don't yell "Can the Kaiser" and "Bound for Berlin" it's no sign I am not in this war heart and soul, body and mind.

Did you know that we got a service stripe for that time down there? Sure enough we did: a little strip signifying "six months military service in Italy," but nobody wears it because we didn't do anything to deserve it and it is very misleading. We also received the eagle representing the Italian Military Brevet, but we don't wear the "Brass Buzzards," as we prefer the R.M.A. (I send one of each.)

Do you get the *Stars and Stripes,* the A.E.F. paper? I sent you a subscription a long time ago. It surely is a fine little paper—not so little either; it's larger than any of the European papers. It contains some excellent descriptions of life in the Amexforce and reflects the fine spirit of the fellows in a way not possible by any other medium. I have also sent you some copies of the *Plane News* published here, which shows what the Air Service is thinking and doing.

Did you ever get the cable I sent from Italy on June 5th? No one has mentioned it and it cost _____. I haven't had any mail from home since I have been here. The last letter was received at Tours and was addressed to Italy, which entails a delay of two weeks. Had a swell letter from May,[2] one from Aunt Blanche,[3] and a couple of George's weekly bulletins. Of course, I know you can't write to all of us every week and I don't want you to tire yourself in the attempt. Reg and I exchange letters regularly.

How's old Tay getting along? Was glad to hear that he

[2]A first cousin, sister of Maurice B. Rowe.

[3]The wife of his uncle, A. P. Rowe.

likes the place in S.C. and the experience away from home will do him lots of good, but experience at school will do infinitely more, provided he comes to his senses. It seems that there is some sort of bugaboo about high school which gets every one of us. Nothing would please me more than to have him go to V.P.I. this year. Don't let him wait; it's fatal, and I bet that he will work like the dickens as soon as he gets into it. V.P.I. is not a kindergarten and I know that he will respond when he feels that he is being treated like a man—none of that 10 hour stuff—and the military will be a tonic to him. He must understand that he has a whole lot to learn and must get over the idea that he can milk a cow just as well now as he can with a college degree. Make him go now. If I had gone straight from high school to college I would have been through last year, but as it is I will have to go back after this is over—and I'm going to. I am not even going to unpack my trunk at home. And I don't think you should let him decide what to do, as he isn't old enough to know, but he is old enough to begin developing his mind. Let me know what you decide to do.

I enclose a letter from Mrs. Whittinghill, and one from my good friend, Miss Spink, of London, whom I met at Capri. These letters I send may be boring to you as you can't appreciate everything in them, but they are rather unusual and are such a treat I thought perhaps you might care to read them. Miss Spink is one of the most interesting and attractive girls I ever met. In fact, all the English men and women that I know are "ripping." They are wonderful people and I want to go to London sometime if I can. I suppose that you know we are using English girls in our offices, English methods, English guns, English uniforms, English aeroplanes, and, as Miss Spink says, "even the English language."

In France

Dear Mother:

Although this has been one of the strenuous six-hour days and I am nearly all in from so much continuous flying, I shall get off some kind of letter to you. Flying requires very little physical effort, but after several hours of it anyone is tired from the constant nervous strain. This may seem queer because after a certain amount of flying an aviator gets so he can do most of his work mechanically, without any special thought, but still he is always keyed up to a high pitch, although at times he may be sailing along calmly, thinking about home and his girl, still he is automatically listening to his motor, watching the altitude gauge and speedometer and feeling and correcting the slightest movement of the plane.

Today I flew in three formations of two hours each and had all kinds of fun. First, three of us went off in a triangular formation, being about 50 yards apart. I was end man on the left. The sky was covered with big white, billowy clouds and we played "follow the leader" while we hunted for openings to get above the clouds. At 5,500 feet we were just skimming the tops and enjoying the most gorgeous sight I have ever witnessed. On every side as far as the eye could reach were these immense, puffy white clouds, intensely bright with the sun gleaming down on them, sunbeams dancing and the air so crisp and pure. Oh! It was just wonderful—like miles of fluffy snowdrifts. Sometimes for ten or fifteen minutes we couldn't see the ground at all and then we would get just a glimpse through an opening in a dense bank.

Everything went well for about an hour, as the leader had a compass and a map, although the latter was of little

113

use to him. Then the fellow on the right broke away and started gliding down, indicating that there was trouble. I followed to see where he landed and make sure that he didn't smash. He got down O.K. and waved me on, but by that time the leader was out of sight. I started off alone to camp and was so confident of the direction that I climbed above the clouds again and when I thought I was directly over the camp I throttled down and dived. Coming out of the clouds I looked all around, but could not locate camp or any familiar landmark, and after cruising around a while without recognizing anything I had to admit that I was lost, and as my gas was getting low I headed for the first thing that looked like a field. I landed in a French camp near _____ and found that while I was above the clouds I had drifted twenty miles off the course. I got my bearings, jollied with the Frenchies a while and then followed a railroad back to my camp with about a pint of gas to spare. The repair truck went out to fix up my comrade who had gone down and in about two hours he flew in. His magneto had broken.

Then I had a formation of three, and although it was still cloudy I managed to pilot them around for two hours and bring them back to camp; but it wasn't my fault. The map was useless and the compass didn't help much on account of the wind. For an hour and a half I knew exactly where I was, but after that things got twisted and I was about to give up in despair when a break in the clouds showed the camp directly below us. Of course, I knew exactly where it was all the time! Yes, I did not. Next we ran off a good diamond-shaped formation without getting lost.

This formation flying is lots of fun, but at the same time it is hard to work, and each one must keep his proper height and distance from the others. The leader has streamers on his struts with which he gives signals. He calls "Attention" and then whatever he does we all follow suit and then look around to see what has become of the others. At first we get scattered all over the sky, but after a little practice the fellows get so they can execute every kind of maneuver with all the precision of a squad of soldiers. After a while we fly in formations of fifteen or twenty and show what we would do to a Hun circus that showed itself.

But I am getting ahead of my story. I finished up my cross-country flying and acrobatics last week and am now on the last stage of training. The two C. C. trips were most interesting, being about forty and sixty miles each way. On the first I flew over a mammoth American plant for assembling airplanes and trucks. It was enormous and a regular city in itself, and there were so many sheds and shops and warehouses that one could not count them all. It took me several minutes to fly around it.

On my second trip I passed over an American infantry camp, where two battalions were going through the interesting exercises of "Squads Right," "March," etc. The temptation was too great, so I swooped down and added a little "Double Time," and maybe that drill was not broken up. I am sure the doughboys themselves didn't mind, but it was lucky for me that I didn't have motor trouble just then, as I would certainly have gotten a royal reprimand from the enraged major.

The course in acrobatics is rather strenuous and covers everything that can be done with a plane—loops, spins, spirals, slips, "renversements," "vrilles" and "virages." They aren't especially hard after a fellow makes up his mind to do them, but we usually put it off as long as possible, then wait two or three minutes longer, think of home, rehearse in our minds what the instructor had told us, figure up our life insurance, curse ourselves for even wanting to fly, remember how our girl looks, take a deep breath and say, "Here goes." In a flash it's all over and one says, "Gee, that's great," and does it again. Then the student comes down, gets out of the machine with a lofty air, struts across the field and tells the other victims what a cinch it is.

I am now at the last training field of the world's largest aviation center and I should be through here in a week. Here we do combat work and if proficient will go to the front as chasse (scout) pilots. Chasse work is the service de luxe of aviation and I count myself lucky to be able to stick this far. I qualified for chasse training and am now getting it and this week will tell whether I make the grade. If I don't succeed I go to the front for reconnaissance, artillery observation, or something else, but the scout work is best of all and every fellow doesn't even get a chance to go this far before being switched, but I am praying for the best. In the combat training work we are given a certain district to patrol and attack every plane that crosses it. It doesn't take long to tell which plane has the better of it and you win out a reasonable number of times. The instructor gives you his O.K. and you go to the front to do real patrols.

These Nieuport planes we use are wonderful little machines and the mechanics keep them in excellent condition. Seldom is there a forced landing on account of motor trouble, but quite a few of the fellows get lost on the cross-country trips, though they never have the slightest difficulty in locating some swell chateau. Many of them get lost (?) and stay out for two or three days, coming back with thrilling tales of Chateau Beautiful and Mademoiselle Charming, and making all the rest of us wish that our motors had gone bad, too.

In France

The funniest thing about aviation is that a pilot is known by the place where he received his training—namely: "Frenchmen," "Italians," of whom I am one, "Americans," and a very few "Englishmen." The Frenchmen and the Italians stand like the Solid South against the recent invasion of the "Americans." Seniority is one reason why we stand aloof from the newcomers. We entered the service before they did and have been over here nearly a year while they are just coming over. The fellows who went through that miserable time last winter as cadets in France and Italy haven't much patience with the fliers coming over now with stories of lots of flying, plenty of good food, dances galore, weekend passes home, and royal treatment all around. Some of them ask, "Where do we get sheets, and is this upper bunk for our trunks?" Such questions make us feel that it is our duty to take them down a peg or two.

Excuse me for boring you with descriptions of flying; it would be much easier to tell you of other things, but there is really nothing else. I haven't been away from camp at all—oh, yes, I have, too. One blistering hot day a bunch of us got a truck and drove ten miles to a little river, where we had the best swim in the world. It was the first time I had been overboard since a dip in the Chesapeake last summer and for once we found something that was as much fun as flying.

Here's hoping for early service at the front.

Devotedly,

Josiah P. Rowe, Jr.

147th Aero Squadron
1st Pursuit Group
American Air Service
France
October 17, 1918

My dearest Mother:

I haven't written for several days, as I was waiting for it to clear up so that I could go over the lines and then have some real news for you, but it is still raining and according to the reputation of France, I'd better not wait for it to stop. During this rainy weather it is impossible to carry out patrols, so all we have to do is to sit around our nice fireplaces, talk about our girls and home and swap stories about flying and every other subject under the sun. Right here I want to sing praises to the man who invented the open fireplace. What a boon to mankind and what a blessing to aviators on rainy days and chilly nights! We have rigged up three comfortable and spacious seats, something like a divan, and in the most luxurious of the three I have established headquarters.

I haven't been over the German lines yet, but I have been in them—that is, what were the German lines a few days ago, and two shells from the German guns have gone off within a hundred yards of me. Here's the story of how I had the unusual opportunity of witnessing from the comfortable seat of a Fiat touring car some of the sights that go to make a regular war. We were out after confirmations, that is, when a pilot brings down a Hun machine he reports it, but is not given credit until it is confirmed. Usually there is another pilot who witnesses the combat, but sometimes there is no one present and then the pilot has to go out in search of someone who saw the engagement. In most cases our balloons can furnish the necessary data and it was upon this mission that I saw a good deal of what war looks like.

We left about 10 A.M., traveling over some of those wonderful roads like boulevards—"the roads that saved France"—and on them you see a spectacle that impresses you with the immensity of this war more than anything else. How are the millions of men at the front supplied with food, clothing, munitions and equipment? There's the answer right before you—motor trucks. There they go—trucks, trucks, trucks by the thousands; trucks of every kind, size and description carrying every conceivable thing from soldiers to sardines. Big Packard trucks, little Ford trucks, heavy French trucks, trucks driven by Americans, Frenchmen, Chinese, Senegalese, East Indians, South Africans; ambulances driven by Red Cross girls, motorcycles darting in and out of the line, touring cars skirting around and forging ahead—thus it goes all day and all night in an endless procession, going up one side of the road and coming back on the other. It is positively bewildering to me to think of where they all go and it seems impossible that one mastermind is directing that never ending stream of traffic and that every wheel that turns does so according to carefully laid plans. It staggers the mind to think that all this hurry and scurry, the chugging of motors and tooting of horns, every driver intent upon his own particular mission, is going on all the time so that our soldiers may have their food promptly and our guns be always supplied with shells.

At every corner and fork in the road is an American and French military policeman to direct and control the traffic. The Frenchman always waits to see which way the American waves his hand, then very gravely motions the same way.

After a while we were going over roads where the traffic was much lighter, trucks were very few, and horses and mule-drawn vehicles taking their places. All along there were increasing evidences of our proximity to the scene of active operations: pretty green fields ruined by deep winding trenches which ran across them like an ugly scar; row upon row of barbed wire entanglements; big and little shell holes, half filled with water, on every side; trees with every branch shot away and the trunks shattered. Once in a while we passed through what once was a village, but now there is only a mass of powdered and crumbling stone, with little to show that here a happy and contented people had lived and pretty little children had played their innocent games in the streets and about the public square. Some of the blasted towns reminded me of Pompeii and some of an abandoned stone quarry.

Farther along we passed thousands of American engineers hard at work rebuilding the roads and bridges—"manicuring boulevards" as Reg calls it. Then we passed battery after battery of our artillery and everyone was working away as if each shell was aimed at the Kaiser himself. For miles and miles there were camps of doughboys belonging to reserve divisions and they weren't in nice barracks like they had in the States or in the billets of the training stations over here. They were in little dog tents with such shelter from the rain and mud as they could provide with sticks and branches of trees. Some were living in the dugouts of old trench systems.

Passing these we came upon a section of country that was more barren and desolate looking than any. There were long hills running parallel and between them a fairly level stretch of about two miles. Both hills and nearly all of the valley were honeycombed with trenches and the barbed wire was so thick that one could hardly walk through it. There was hardly a square foot of ground in all this area that had not been torn up with shells. Guess where this was? No other place than "Hill 304" or "Dead Man's Hill," about which there was such terrible fighting in 1916 when the Germans were driving on Verdun. The French were entrenched on the hill to the south and the Germans occupied the hill to the north. The middle space was swept by fire from both sides. It was across this plain that the German "waves" advanced and were checked with such deadly effect by the French "75s" and machine guns. The situation, both topographically and tactically, was remarkably similar to the Battle of Fredericksburg, but Fredericksburg, at its very worst, could never have presented such a picture of desolation. There was not one living thing in sight—not an animal of any kind, not even a bush— just a barren waste, broken only by shell holes, trenches and barbed wire. It seemed incredible that once upon a time people lived there, had their little farms and gardens and cows and chickens. It gave me a shiver to think of the awful carnage that took place there, and I was glad to get away from such gruesome scenes.

At another place we went into some German trenches which had only recently been captured by the Americans. There were piles of cartridge cases, machine gun belts, hand and rifle grenades, clothing and supplies on every side, all going to show that the Huns had left rather hurriedly. Like every other real American I wanted a souvenir so I picked up a very nice looking hand grenade and was thinking about how nice it would look hanging over a mantlepiece when my comrade reminded me that hand grenades were often "fixed" by the Germans to go off as soon as touched by some such gink as I. Maybe I didn't let it drop, but before it struck the ground I remembered that they were set off by percussion. I looped the loop into a friendly trench and crouched in suspense for a while, then came out and "swore off" on souvenirs.

Later we went through Verdun itself or rather what was left of it. One side of the city is completely demolished, but the other isn't nearly as bad, as the houses are only partly wrecked and some of them actually have a part of the roof left. One building looked fairly habitable, having three walls intact and the front door only half shot away. The streets are passable, thanks to the American engineers, but the sidewalks are littered with wreckage and debris. Speaking of making the Germans restore the ruined towns, they can never restore Verdun or any of the wrecked villages we saw.

While in Verdun, two German shells whizzed over our heads, struck and exploded uncomfortably near our machine. They weren't carrying on a regular bombardment, but were dropping over a few stray shells whither to worry the troops or else just from force of habit.

Later in the course of our journey we came upon a division coming out of the trenches for "repose" and one glance at the weary, worn faces would show that they needed it. The poor devils were covered with mud, some had no hats, some had no coats, and it was all they could do to drag themselves along the road. I pitied them and also envied them, as they have seen and experienced some things that many never know. At the head of the long column were the wagons and at the head of the wagons were the caissons and at the head of the caissons was— well, just guess. We had a dickens of a time getting past them on a narrow road and twice we got held up in "jams" which threatened to keep us there until dark and heaven help anyone who has to travel through that country at night. We finally reached the head of the column and put on a dash of speed to get clear and right there I nearly fell out of the car. Leading the entire column was one caisson drawn by six horses and sitting on that caisson in a form-fitting suit of O.D. and mud, his brow shaded by the very latest style "tin hat," his feet artistically clad in handsome hobnailed shoes, No. 10 EE, was none other than one of Fredericksburg's most popular young men—the well-known dancer, pool shark and lady killer—Lew Rock. I recognized him at once by his characteristic smile and gave him a yell. He looked once and yelled back. By that time the car had turned a corner and I didn't see him again. I've been kicking myself ever since because I didn't stop, but at the time it didn't seem wise as it was nearly dark and we had about 40 miles to go over bad roads with possibilities of getting caught in other "jams." Gee! But I wish I could have stopped and talked to old Lew again. All I know about him now is his division and there isn't a chance of finding him without something more definite.

There will be many happy reunions after the war and for me, not the least of them will be when I see dear old Lew and kid him to death about being at the head of the division—when it started to the rear.

We got back to camp shortly after dark, bringing with us confirmation of five victories for this group. The First Pursuit Group[1] had 103 victories in September, which is some record. For October we have fog, mist and clouds and rain.

My candle is sputtering its last, so goodnight.

Best love to you and everybody.

Your devoted son,

Josiah

[1]The First Pursuit Group consisted of five aero squadrons: the 27th, 94th, 95th, 147th and 185th.

147th Aero Squadron
France
Nov. 1, 1918

My dearest Mother:

Things are happening so fast and exciting events are so frequent that I'll have to start writing to you in short-hand if I am going to keep pace with them. The weather for the past four days has certainly been magnificent, permitting great aerial activity, and the First Pursuit Group has been on the jump. Capt. Rickenbacker[1] has gotten two balloons and a Fokker; Capt. Meissner,[2] two balloons, and numerous other pilots have scored victories during the break in the weather. Day before yesterday the various pursuit squadrons brought down 21 Huns, which is a pretty good day's work. Capt. Meissner, my C.O., gave us quite a scare the other night—he left just before dark to attack a certain balloon and two hours later, when nothing had been heard of him, we began to be worried and as time passed our anxiety increased. He came in about 9 o'clock on a truck, having had a forced landing just before he reached the lines and was unable to get to a telephone. While all these glorious things are going on, I am "carrying on" at the same old job—waiting. Now I am waiting for a plane. Had one once but couldn't fly on account of the weather, then when it did clear up, one of the old men had

[1]Capt. Edward V. Rickenbacker, commanding officer of the 94th Aero Squadron, was credited with shooting down 26 enemy aircraft in two months, making him the most victorious American aviator and earning him recognition as the country's ace of aces (an ace was an aviator with five or more aerial combat victories).

[2]Major James Armand Meissner, commanding officer of the 147th Aero Squadron and an ace with eight victories.

a crash and I had to give it up. I left the States over a year ago and still haven't done the thing that I came over for, but I haven't given up hope yet. One of the old men, who is a particular friend of mine, has promised to be sick tomorrow so I can use his machine and with good weather I will be able to make my debut over the lines. The big drive that we have been expecting for several days is on, and I am going to take part in it if I have to commit murder in order to do it, as this may be the last drive and I don't want to get left out in the cold.

The most interesting thing that has happened since I last wrote you was a de luxe trip up to the front lines. The other day we got a report that Hun planes were coming down below our patrols and shooting up our troops. This sounded fishy as we are out there to prevent that very thing, and as our patrols are carried out at from 300 to 600 metres they couldn't very well be underneath us and our pilots fail to see them. Anyhow, the C.O. detailed three of us to go up and see what was going on, so, comfortably seated in his Packard touring car, we sailed away to "See the War."

We came up to an anti-aircraft battery just in time to see seven Fokkers at 2,500 metres chasing two of our observation planes. Several batteries opened upon them as soon as they got within range and made it so hot that they broke up the formation and beat it back to their side of the lines. These Archies seldom hit anything, in fact they don't expect to, but they can make things mighty unpleasant for the pilot. Occasionally we have planes come back with shrapnel holes in their wings.

Then we went on farther, past batteries of artillery, mountains of ammunition, and regiments of doughboys. We ran past our balloon line and knew we were getting pretty close to the advanced lines, but no shells were coming over so we kept on; through a village recently captured from the Germans in which the Boche signboards and street names were still standing; past infantry in dugouts with helmets on and gas masks ready for use, and came to a town pretty well shot to pieces. We looked for an M.P. to ask for directions but there were no M.P.'s; we looked for anyone who could give us information but the place was absolutely deserted. We backed up the road to a group of doughboys standing in a dugout and asked for an M.P. "No, sir, I don't know where you'll find one." "Well, isn't there anyone here to regulate traffic?" "Hell no! There ain't no traffic up here." It developed that this was our second line trench and no vehicle ever came up there during the day. Just then a wounded soldier came limping along and we took him in for a lift. He said he had walked from the front line trench and, when asked how far they were, said "Oh! They're right down at the foot of that hill."

Can you imagine that? Being within a quarter of a mile of the front lines and not knowing it? And in a Packard car at that? We weren't concerned at all about our own safety as we were too deeply interested to think of any danger but we were afraid that the Boche might begin shelling at any minute and damage that Packard so we began a strategic retreat and took the doughboy to a field hospital.

While there, three Fokkers came over pretty high up and headed towards two of our observation balloons which were anchored at 500 metres. Two of the Huns stayed above for protection and the third dived down at one of the balloons shooting with both machine guns. The observers jumped out in parachutes and the Archies and machine guns on the ground started peppering away at the Fokker, raising a terrific racket. He failed to set fire to the balloon and began climbing towards Germany, dodging shrapnel puffs and zigzagging to evade machine gun bullets. Just then two Spads came tearing up and we saw by the insignia that they were from our squadron. They made for the Fokker which quit circling and headed full speed towards its own lines with the Spads hot after it. The two Huns up above started back also and they had a fine opportunity to swoop down on the Spads but they never attack unless they have two or three to one. Later, we found out that our pilots followed the retreating Hun for several miles and shot it down. Lt. O'Neil,[3] of Arizona, got the credit for it.

After nosing around for some time, during which I met several artillery officers who were in my battery at Fort Myer, making inquiries and answering questions about how everyone there could get into the Air Service, we took a road that ran parallel to the Front and followed it for about thirty miles. All this territory had recently been held by the Germans but had been captured by the Yanks. The country had been fought over so much that there was little left but trenches, barbed wire and shell holes. Every inch of roadway had been or was being rebuilt by our hardworking engineers. All along were piles of captured stores consisting of guns, ammunition, gas masks, hand grenades, trench mortars, etc., and in one place there was an immense quantity of steel breastplates which the Huns have been using. We saw lots of aerial activity and several combats but they were all so high that we couldn't tell much about them. On the way back we passed through Verdun again and had several more shells fall very near us. The Boche can't seem to get out of the habit of shelling that battered city.

Our trip confirmed our belief that there was nothing to

[3]1st Lt. Ralph Ambrose O'Neil, a six-victory ace.

the report about Hun planes attacking our infantry. We didn't see anything like it and questioned everything from colonels to K.P.'s but they only knew of isolated cases which are apt to happen at any time. It's funny how much respect we commanded all along the line—lieutenants, captains and once a major came sharply to attention and saluted—the Packard.

The next day three of us were selected to go in an automobile to an air depot[4] about 75 miles back to get some new planes, one of which was to be mine. I called up Reg and asked him if he wanted to go but he couldn't get away. The planes weren't ready that day so we went over to a well known city to spend the night, getting there just in time for supper and an air raid. When the "alerte" sounded, all the Frenchmen ran to the "abris"[5] and all the Americans ran to the street where they could see what was going on. It was a most spectacular sight with the town in inky blackness; about a dozen flashlights playing across the heavens; the flash and crack of exploding shrapnel; and the terrific boom and crash of the bombs which fell at regular intervals making the earth tremble like a leaf; and above it all the hum of the Hun motor. Fifteen bombs were dropped, one striking a building on our block, completely demolishing it. We were darn fools to stand out in the open like that with shrapnel raining all around and stones and fragments flying in every direction but it was the first air raid we had experienced and we couldn't afford to miss any of it. Now that I have been in one I don't care for any more. Of course you are the center of the universe and every bomb is aimed directly at you. I defy any man to go through a bombing raid without showing a decided increase in heart action.

[4]In Colombey-les-Belles.

[5]An air raid shelter, often built into the side of a hill.

In spite of the excitement caused by the air raid we succeeded in getting a good supper, a good bath and a good bed. The next morning there was a dense fog so we decided to go back to camp as the C.O. might want to use his car once in a while. We stopped at Red Cross Hqtrs. and asked for the two girls who are coming up to operate a canteen for us and make life worth living. They are corking fine girls and we begged them to come with us but they weren't quite ready.

I saw Dick Moncure, of Stafford, who is on M.P. duty, and talked with him a while. He is looking fine and seems to be getting along nicely. Didn't have time to talk to him very long but it surely was good to see a familiar face. If it's a good day tomorrow I'll probably go back after a plane.

Had the good fortune to visit Reg again last week and spend a day and night with the old kid. Went over in the afternoon, dragged him off to a little village for supper but we came mighty near not getting any because of an air raid on a nearby town which had everyone so excited and scared that it was all we could do to make them attend to business long enough to fry some eggs and make the coffee. For the same reason we couldn't get a room, so we walked back to camp where Reg found an extra cot and a couple of blankets for me. I stayed with him until the following afternoon and then bummed rides on trucks back to camp. I took along my camera in the hopes that it might clear up long enough for us to get a picture but no such luck. He is coming over to spend a day and night with me pretty soon.

On Oct. 27th I put on my second service stripe indicating one year with the A.E.F. It seems like four years since that Saturday afternoon when we sailed from New York. I was certainly blue that day when starting off to war without a soul in the world to say good-bye to. According to the *Stars and Stripes* there are only one hundred thousand "two-stripers" which makes me one of the First Hundred Thousand Americans in France. I'll probably get another stripe yet but I'd much rather get a ticket home.

What do you think of the peace dope? Things look mighty good to me and it's a pretty sure thing that the boys will be "out of the trenches" by Xmas. Bets of every kind are being placed on every important question—when peace will be declared; who will get home first; who will get married first, etc., etc. I'll bet anybody 50 francs that no one in France wants to get home any worse than I do. Since the latest American advance we can't hear the guns any more but no one wants to hear them and I hope in a very short time they won't. You can go up in the garret some one of these days and get out such of my "cits" as Taylor hasn't annexed.

Drop a line and tell me all about everything—what Hanny[6] is doing—who Taylor is going to see—the name of Julia Mason's latest piece of music—etc. My best love to everybody and best wishes for a joyous and happy Thanksgiving.

Lovingly, your son—

Josiah

[6]Hansford Herndon Rowe, a brother (1893–1945).

In France

147th Aero Squadron
France
November 8, 1918

My dearest Mother and All:

Well, thank heaven, I'm not a rookie any more, I have seen real, active service—yes, very real and active. At last I have a plane of my own[1] and am now doing regular patrols over the German lines. "What is it like?" I can hear you asking now. Well, here it is from the start.

You get your orders the night before so that your slumbers will be a perfect nightmare of home and forced landings, your sweetheart and Fokkers and all your friends. Then next morning[2] you get your motor warmed up, try out your guns, look around and say "so long" to the mechanics. The latter are fine fellows and it hurts them as much as anyone when a pilot goes out and doesn't come back and you fervently hope that you won't cause them any pain. Then you cross your fingers, pull open the throttle and take off, circle around the field a couple of times, take up your place in the formation and set out towards the lines.

You are flying along at 300 meters (a nice altitude—on this side) and the country below is just like any other, with fields and forests and farms, but you don't think of it that way at all. Here is an aerodrome from which planes are leaving, there is a camp with scenes of great activity; on one road is a long line of artillery moving up, on another a convoy of trucks coming back.

[1]The plane was a Spad XIII, #15239.

[2]On November 7, 1918, a voluntary patrol in the region of Mouzon-Steney was led by "C" Flight Commander 2nd Lt. Kenneth Lee Porter (a five-victory ace) and was composed of 1st Lt. Francis May Simonds, Jr. (also a five-victory ace) and Josiah.

131

You notice scenes like this for a few moments, then the whole thing gradually changes; you pass over Verdun, which as usual is being shelled and which about makes the end of the first reel. The country is different now, the villages have been shattered, the forests have been shot away, the once green fields are a sickly brown covered with shell craters and irregular lines of trenches, which look like ugly scars. There is artillery, but it is heavily camouflaged, and intermittent flashes show that it is in action; instead of motor trucks there are wagons and carts. Then you pass our sausage balloons and before you know it you have crossed the lines and are over German territory.

How do you know this? Geographically or topographically you can't tell just when you go "over the top," but shellographically you know well that Germans are below you. All at once a number of black puffs appear around you and you notice that the leader is "S–ing" violently. You start "S–ing" too and just when you have cut a sharp circle to the left you hear a crack and another black puff appears just off the tip of your wing. Pretty close when you can hear the report above the noise of your motor, but you can imagine a Boche gunner is cursing because he missed you. From then on you keep continuously twisting and turning, leaving behind you a trail of the wicked-looking black puffs.

Down below you can see groups of Huns; some in trenches, some behind a clump of bushes, some creeping up a road. All around is the smoke from our shells and the Boche seem to be laying low to avoid them. There is one group of Huns poorly concealed under a clumsy piece of camouflage, and while you look, a stream of sparks come out headed in your direction—incendiary and explosive bullets from a machine gun. Pretty bum, but he is correcting his aim; you nose over, kick your rudder to get a good aim, and pull both triggers; looks like the Fourth of July with one gun firing incendiaries and one spaced with tracers. You can see your shots going into their midst; they cease firing and scatter—some don't!!! You pull up and rejoin the formation.

You have orders to attack balloons and low flying Hun planes, but none of either are visible. Way off on the horizon you see a black speck and wonder what it is. Maybe it's a balloon and your leader is going after it. No, it's a plane all right and it is coming toward you, but what kind is it? Hun or Allied? If it's a Hun he will be easy; it's a two-seater and much slower than our Spads. He gets closer and you grip your triggers, but just then he tips up his wing and shows the American insignia. Oh, yes; it's a Liberty taking pictures and you wave as it goes past.

Then you look up and get the surprise of your life. Seven Fokkers directly above you at about 1,000 meters, their black crosses and brightly colored bodies plainly visible. Good Lord! How long have they been there and how long before they are going to swoop down on you—seven of them and only three of you. You instinctively edge in closer to the leader and wonder if he has seen them too. Yes, he has and begins climbing into the sun, but it's no use. They are watching and start climbing too, and we can never catch them. The leader swings off and starts toward the other end of our patrol; they turn and follow. Then comes the agonizing suspense when you expect them to tumble down on you at any moment. Then you almost run into a Salmson[3] (French-American) directing artillery fire. So that's what the bloody Fokkers are after and they won't come down because you are there.

Then you look at your watch to see if it isn't about time to go home—9 minutes since you left Verdun, and

[3]An airplane.

you have to stay an hour and a half. Well, you just stay with a repetition of what I have told you and with this added: all this time you have one eye on the Fokkers above, one eye on your leader, one eye behind for Huns that might try to surprise you and one eye on your instruments to see that everything is all right. Your motor is running sweetly, but you never can tell, and if it ever once misses or sputters your heart stops dead; you are six or seven kilometers within the German lines and you can't possibly reach our side. Thoughts of a German prison camp aren't very agreeable. With good luck and a tail wind you may reach No Man's Land and make a run for it, but no matter which side you land on you may be sure of a crash, for there is nothing in sight but trenches, shellholes and barbed wire. You may be thinking of your girl and what you are going to tell her when you get back, but the chances are that you are hoping to heaven that your magnetos won't cut out on you and that your radiator won't spring a leak.

Eventually, the leader swings off and starts toward home; you heave a sigh of relief and relax when you cross the Meuse River, which is only about half again as large as Hazel Run.[4] Then you remember the bundle of newspapers which you have brought along and you pick out a bunch of doughboys, glide down to within about 30 feet of them and toss them out. It's worth a million dollars just to see them scramble and wave to us as we circle above. Then you head for home, humming a little snatch of "Madelon" and wondering what you will have for supper.

When you get back, the mechanics run out to meet you and ask how the plane is running and if you did any running. You climb out and tell them in a bored sort of way that the plane is all right, but that there wasn't much

[4]A stream in Fredericksburg that flows into the Rappahannock River.

doing over the lines, just a few "Archies"[5] and a bunch of Fokkers, but really nothing to speak of—nothing at all.

So far I have only been on two patrols, the first being as above described. On the second[6] we had orders to "strafe" a road leading out of a certain town. There were four of us and we gave them—what several fellows back home told me to give them. The Huns were evacuating and the road was jammed with trucks, guns, and columns of troops. We went over at 400 metres and dived on them, shooting to beat the band. You should have seen the mess that we created. Trucks ran into each other and ran off the road, troops ran in every direction, horses stampeded and a regular havoc resulted. Some few fired back at us but missed. It takes some crack shot to hit an aeroplane going along at 140 miles an hour—more than that when diving. We had a terrific A.A.[7] barrage, but were lucky enough to get through it unhurt.

We didn't see a single Hun plane or balloon on this trip and at this rate I haven't got much chance of getting "Mine." I'm sure I got a number of Huns in that "road strafing" expedition, but they don't count and I'm wild to get one in the air. All the old men in the squadron have four or five Boches to their credit and recently a number have been awarded the D.S.C. and the Croix de Guerre. I've got to get a Hun some way or other and I've got to do it quick because it looks now as if we may have peace almost any day.

During the last week two very charming Red Cross girls have joined the group and are operating the dandiest

[5]Antiaircraft guns.

[6]On November 10, 1918, a patrol to strafe retreating enemy troops was led by 1st Lt. Walter Paul Muther and was composed of 1st Lt. James Patrick Herron, 1st Lt. Charles E. Cox and Josiah. Cox aborted early due to propeller trouble.

[7]Antiaircraft.

little rest room and canteen in France. They have a nice little shack with curtains on the windows, covers on the table, cushions on the chairs, wood on the fire, and a teakettle on the stove. They serve tea, chocolate, cookies, and candy every afternoon, which is very delightful, but the C.O. threatens to close it up on the grounds that the pilots are always late for patrols. It surely is fine and last night while I was there I really had a glimpse of home. I was there writing letters (or trying to) in company with a number of others. The others must have had early morning patrols for most of them left early, leaving only me and two others. (Couldn't possibly shake these two.) Pretty soon one of the girls came in, drew up a rocking chair before the fireplace and began knitting. (Immediately cessation of correspondence.) We all talked for a while and then just sat and gazed into the fire. I give you my word that in five minutes she was asleep with her knitting hanging down to the floor. I didn't need to close my eyes to picture the well-known sitting room scene at home, even though we didn't have Black Joe curled up before the fire, and Julia Mason working algebra problems and Papa talking about the Civil War. Twice I unconsciously started to put out the cat and wind up the clock and I almost made the awful (nice) mistake of kissing her goodnight.

I am going to fly over to see Reg in a day or two. Goodnight.

Your devoted son,

Josiah

147th Aero Squadron
1st Pursuit Group
France
November 29, 1918

My dearest Mother:

What would you think if I told you that I had met about a dozen Fredericksburgers all in one day? No doubt you would say that I was dreaming—things like that don't often happen in France, but it really is true. If you don't believe it ask me how Miss Grace Morrison looks in her nurse's uniform, how Dr. Pratt and Dr. Sale look in overseas caps, and how Dr. Guy Hopkins looks as a captain. This isn't a fairytale at all—this is how it happened: "Voila." Some days ago a letter for Reg was delivered to me by mistake and, of course, I took the liberty of opening it. It was from Miss Grace Morrison giving her address as Base Hospital No. 45, A.P.O. 784, which meant nothing at all to me, because I did not know the location of the hospital. I stuck the letter in my pocket, intending to give it to Reg the next time I saw him.

The next day I had to fly an old ship to Colombey-les-Belles (our supply depot) and get a new one in exchange. Started back in a nice plane with the motor running like a dream. Flew over the city of Toul and had a good look at it and the large number of hospitals located there. I was sailing along merrily and was thinking of stopping to see Reg on my way. About ten miles past Toul the radiator sprung a leak and the temperature started up like a balloon. I happened to be right over an aerodrome, so I landed and asked them to fix me up. They said it wouldn't be finished until the next day and it seemed I was condemned to spend the night in a very small village which knew of no such thing as a hotel. Just then a French lieutenant landed with a broken water pump which could not be repaired. He went into town and conferred with some French officers and wheedled an auto out of them with which to go back to his aerodrome at Nancy. Nancy sounded good to me, so I invited myself to go along. We went to the field, got a new pump, and decided to spend the night in town. Had a corking good supper, went to a show and got good rooms in a hotel. Incidentally, Nancy is quite a live town, was all lit up like a church and just covered with decorations. (Of course you are wondering just what all this has to do with Miss Grace Morrison—but wait.)

Next morning the Frenchman and I started back in the car, but when we got to Toul it began raining like the dickens, so I decided to stay there until it cleared up. It was then that the great idea came to me and just on a wild chance I asked an M.P. what the A.P.O. number was. When he said 784, I asked where Base Hospital 45 was and started on a run. It wasn't more than ¼ mile and I made it in nothing flat. I dashed right up to the head nurse and introduced myself. I didn't ask her *if* I could see Miss Grace, but "*Where* is Miss Grace?" She said that Miss Grace was on night duty and could not be disturbed in the day time. She was very firm about it, but I kidded her along and told her that she reminded me of _____ who was a most charming woman. She fell for it and told me to wait in the recreation room. In about four minutes Miss Grace came in. My! But I was glad to see her and she didn't seem half mad to find me, although I think she expected to find some medical lieutenant, who is looking forward to the days of "après le guerre." We talked and talked and talked about everything under the sun until dinner time. Then I had a wonderful dinner with about fifty girls from Virginia. Can you beat that? You certainly cannot—in France.

After dinner we went calling and met Dr. Pratt and also Dr. Sale, who was likewise visiting, having just come in from the front. Dr. Pratt has one of the best little mustaches in France—one that would make any Frenchman envious. Dr. Sale is also looking fine. We were standing there talking just as if we had been on a certain corner in Fredericksburg, when Magnus Lewis came up and joined the party. He is also the owner of a dainty little mustache, which rivals Dr. Pratt's (but you ought to see mine!).

After swapping rumors about going home we went in to see Dr. Guy Hopkins. He has charge of the laboratories as he promptly explained and demonstrated by showing me through all his rooms filled with microscopes, test tubes, reports, etc. Everything that he had done, was doing, or expected to do in his experiments with various diseases was explained by the aid of complicated charts, diagrams and pictures. The names of all the germs were pointed out to me with a detailed account of all their habits and characteristics. I thought he must have mistaken me for someone else and started to climb out of the window. Finally he let up on his beloved germs and began asking several thousand questions about aviation. He and all his assistants were putting me through a lengthy cross-examination and I never would have gotten away but for Mag Lewis. In the meantime I had told Miss Grace good-bye so she could go back to sleep.

Mag was off duty and it was still raining, so we decided to go to Nancy for the night. Walked into Toul and saw Lewis Moncure, who was off duty and said he would go with us. Then we went just outside of town and saw John Lanier, who is in a balloon company, and tried to get him to go over to Nancy for a big celebration. He couldn't get off so we stayed there and had a good gumming match for an hour or so. Later Lewis Moncure found that he couldn't get a pass, so Mag and I went on together. Had a peach of a time and returned to Toul the next morning.

Seeing so many folks from home at one time nearly took my breath away and made me feel almost as if I had been in Fredericksburg for a day. Besides all those I have just mentioned I just missed seeing Frank Shelton, of Princess Anne Street, who had been in the hospital until that day when he was evacuated; Wallace Piercy, who was in John Lanier's company, but was away for the day and Karl Pritchett, who is on M.P. duty in Toul. Everyone I saw was looking splendid, as though army grub and German bombs (Toul used to be raided quite often) fully agreed with them. Toul is only about 69 kilos from here and I am certainly going to fly down there some day soon and see them all again. Base Hospital 45 has been in Toul for over three months and I have been there at least a dozen times but never knew before that it was Dr. McGuire's unit from Richmond.

Later I flew back to camp. Had a pretty good Thanksgiving. Fire's out and I am too cold to write more.

Goodnight.

Love,

Josiah

In France

147th Aero Squadron
France
December 7, 1918

My dearest Mother:

Listen, listen, listen!! After a month of uncertainty and confusion we have at last received orders to start for home. HOME—HOME—There's something familiar about that name—seems to me I've heard it before somewhere. I can hardly sit still long enough to write but it's so good I must tell you about it. We start tomorrow and our first move is to go to an air depot near Toul, where we turn in all our equipment and then _____, it's a guess. Maybe it's Bordeaux and a boat for home and maybe it's weeks of waiting in a muddy camp. Anyhow we are starting and that's something. In case of the former there is just the barest chance that we will get home by Christmas and such a Christmas it will be. I am afraid to hope for too much as I may be bitterly disappointed, still there's a chance. Hang up a stocking for me anyhow.

We leave in our planes tomorrow and I am going to say "so long" to Reg and will fly over Hospital 45 and drop a note to Grace Morrison. If we stay near Toul for any length of time I'll be able to see her frequently. Reg was going to Toul today and said he was going to see her.

I spent the night with Reg a few nights ago in the little town of Ligny, near which he is located. Also talked to him over the phone yesterday. He doesn't know anything definite about moving yet.

Reg told me the awful news of Jim Hawkins' death from pneumonia, which completely took my breath away. Only a few days ago I wrote to Margaret and told her to send me his address and I would try to go to see him. It certainly is terrible and I know they are about crushed. Please tell Mrs. Hawkins and Margaret how deeply I sympathize with them.

There isn't a thing around camp of any interest and if it was it would be spoiled by the prospects of going home and of getting there by Christmas or New Year's.

Oh, by the way, Reg and I had planned to go to Verdun today and take some pictures but he had to go to Toul instead. It rained anyhow.

So long, dear Mother. Hope to see you about the time this letter gets there.

Devotedly,

Josiah

Addenda

Excerpts from Josiah's *Officer's Record Book*

All officers below the rank of major were required to carry an official *Officer's Record Book*. The following statements were written in Josiah's book by his commanding officer and flight commander respectively:

> From Oct. 10, 1918, when Lt. Rowe joined the squadron, to Nov. 11, 1918, when the armistice was signed, Lt. Rowe carried out the regular patrols of the squadron over the lines. His work was always well done and he was well thought of by both officers and men.
>
> F. M. Simonds
> 1st Lt. ASUSA[1]
> Commanding 147 AS

> Lt. Rowe joined the squadron Oct. 10, 1918, and from that date flew in many patrols of the lines when the discontinuance of hostile operations on Nov. 11, 1918, put a stop to all patrols. He is a very good pilot and well liked by both officers and men.
>
> Lt. Kenneth L. Porter
> Flight Commander

[1]Air Service, United States Army.

An Overview of the U.S. Air Service During World War I

by Col. Clarence Richard Glasebrook, USAF

When the United States entered the war on 6 April 1917 the Army Signal Corps Aviation Section consisted of 65 officers, 35 of whom were pilots, and 55 aircraft, of which 51 were obsolete and four were obsolescent by combat standards of the day. As the country commenced to mobilize for war, huge sums of money were appropriated to expand military aviation. The U.S. Army immediately started pilot training and aircraft and airfield construction programs. The most successful by far was the pilot training program. Eight American universities were selected to establish Schools of Military Aeronautics. The ground school courses of instruction were to run for eight weeks and teach the rudimentary essentials determined necessary to master in order to become an airplane pilot. These courses were copied almost directly from the Royal Air Force training syllabus.

After completion of ground school, graduates then advanced to flying training. Unfortunately, the construction of airfields and training planes in the United States could not keep pace with the flood of flying cadets being graduated from the ground schools. Our Allies were queried as to their ability to provide flying training for some of these men, and the British, French and Italian governments responded that they could provide some training in limited numbers. Accordingly, as cadets graduated from ground school, some 100 per month were sent to the American

Expeditionary Forces for training at English, French and Italian airfields. Again, a backlog occurred in the ambitious training programs accepted by our Allies and many of these honor graduates of the various Schools of Military Aeronautics who were chosen to be trained overseas were trapped in the old military "hurry up and wait" system.

This delay caused many problems, one of the most serious of which had to do with commissioning and rank. Originally, enlistees were promised, upon successful completion of the primary flying training program, that they would be commissioned first lieutenants. As the numbers of trainees in the pipeline built up, many senior officers in the old Army objected to the procedure, and commissions of second lieutenants were offered instead. To add insult to injury, hundreds of honor graduates of the Schools of Military Aeronautics cooled their heels in concentration camps in Europe awaiting a flying billet in a training school, while some of their lower classmen, who were fortunate enough to be assigned to state-side training fields, earned their pilot wings and commissions and started showing up in numbers at the 3rd Aviation Instruction Center to receive advanced combat training. The issue finally came to the attention of the Secretary of War, and a position was adopted that those cadets who had completed ground school prior to 20 October 1917 would be commissioned as first lieutenants, and those who completed ground school later were to be commissioned second lieutenants immediately and given the option of serving as ground officers if they did not successfully complete flying training.

Some of the more fortunate were able to join British and French squadrons before American squadrons were available to accept them after flight training. Most, like Josiah Rowe, did not graduate from flying training until mid-1918. By this time the American Expeditionary Forces Air Service Headquarters had established a policy that each graduate of preliminary flying school must attend advanced combat flying training at the 3rd Aviation Instruction Center, Issoudun, France, and one of the aerial gunnery schools. This imposed additional delays so that the programmed buildup of American squadrons at the front did not gain momentum until the start of the Meuse-Argonne campaign.

It is noteworthy that of some 11,000 pilots trained by the U.S. Army, a little over one-third were to get to Europe before the end of the war; but of these, only some 600 saw combat. Josiah Pollard Rowe was one of those 600 who through perseverance and good fortune were able to serve their country as Americans in American uniforms flying in American combat squadrons.

Col. Glasebrook was a military historian with a special interest in World War I aviators. With 32 years of service in the Air Force, he served in World War II, the Korean conflict and the Vietnam War, where he flew in over 140 combat missions. A much-decorated veteran, Col. Glasebrook was president of the Glasebrook Foundation for the preservation of military aviation history, which published American Aviators in the Great War, 1914–1918 *in 1984.*

"On the way from Cazaux to the Front." Josiah (at right) had been at Cazaux for aerial gunnery training.

Above is the Spad XIII that Josiah flew in combat patrols in France, and below, Josiah in the cockpit.

1st Lt. Francis Simonds, commanding officer of the 147th Aero Squadron (A.S.), a five-victory ace.

1st Lt. Ken Porter, Josiah's flight commander at Rembercourt, also a five-victory ace.

Capt. Eddie Rickenbacker with a Spad XIII. Rickenbacker was a fellow pilot with Josiah in the First Pursuit Group and was the most successful American combat ace of the war with twenty-six victories.

1st Lt. Charles Cox who had met Josiah's brother, Charles, in Wisconsin before the war.

2nd Lt. Charles "Pip" Porter, "A" Flight Commander in the 147th A.S., a four-victory ace.

2nd Lt. John Stevens of the 147th A.S.

A squadron of planes at Toul.

"This is the Hannover—a German two-seater which we captured intact. Note the dummy, which was used in making a movie of an aerial combat."

"Another view of the Fokker [a German plane that had also been captured, ed.]—a vicious looking thing."

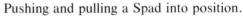

Pushing and pulling a Spad into position.

A plane's machine guns.

2nd Lt. James A. Meissner of the 147th A.S. — an eight-victory ace — in front of a plane in Capt. Rickenbacker's "Hat in the Ring" squadron. The fabric has peeled off the top wing, a common result of a steep dive.

2nd Lt. W. W. White, an eight-victory ace who was killed in action when he deliberately crashed his Spad into a Fokker that was diving at a plane flown by 1st Lt. Charles Cox, and thereby saved his squadronmate's life.

Heavy artillery in France.

At left, the grave of 1st Lt. Quentin Roosevelt, U.S. Air Service, who was killed in action in France. He was the son of former President Teddy Roosevelt. At right, an "abri" or bomb shelter in France.

"Powder magazine, Verdun."

At the Front in Verdun.

Troop and equipment movements
in France.

Destruction at the Front and behind the lines.

The devastation of war.

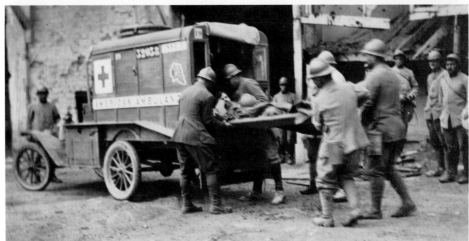

Ambulances in France.

The staff car (a Packard) of the 147th A.S., driven by 1st Lt. James A. Meissner, later to become a major and commanding officer of the 147th.

Soldier in gas mask.

A "captured" German sign.

Doughboys.

At the Front.

This photograph appears to be of a victory parade in Paris where Josiah spent time before returning to America.

AMERICAN FLIERS IN ITALY REUNITE AT CITY HALL

Mayor LaGuardia is one of the Foggiani, an organization of American aviators who trained at Foggia, Italy, for action in the World War. Yesterday afternoon about 100 of the Foggiani called on the Mayor, who is shown above, as Joseph (sic) Rowe, another flier of the Foggia training camp days, pins an identification tag on him. All had lunch together, celebrating then and last night their third reunion since the armistice. *February 20, 1936*

Seventeenth Annual Aviators' Ball

Benefit of

AVIATORS' WELFARE AND RELIEF FUND

Friday evening, February 21, 1936

10:00 P. M.

HOTEL PIERRE

Fifth Avenue, New York City

Table Reservations
and Supper
$7.50 per Couple

Address Remittances
L. B. HAZZARD
110 William St., New York